Learning to Depolarize

How can schools shoulder some responsibility for depolarizing our fractured American society? In this provocative new book, Kent Lenci describes how educators can tackle the challenge of preparing students to communicate and collaborate across lines of deep disagreement—to face the political and ideological "other"—despite the conventional wisdom that schools should be apolitical.

Topics covered include the causes and consequences of political polarization in our society, why schools must address the challenge head-on, bridge-building in the classroom, media literacy and social emotional learning as tools for depolarization, and partnering with parents across the divide.

Each chapter offers current research as well as practical strategies and classroom anecdotes. Appropriate for teachers of all grade levels and subject areas, the book will help you reconsider your classroom and school's role in forging a more depolarized future.

Kent Lenci has been an educator for more than 20 years, as a teacher, coach, and school leader at the middle school level. He is the recipient of the Margot Stern Strom Teaching Award from Facing History and Ourselves and the Teacher of the Future designation from the National Association of Independent Schools. Kent founded Middle Ground School Solutions, which is dedicated to helping schools honor political and ideological differences. He can be reached through his website: www.midd legroundschools.com.

Also Available from Routledge Eye On Education
(www.routledge.com/k-12)

Close Reading the Media: Literacy Lessons and Activities for Every Month of the School Year
Frank Baker

Creating Citizens: Teaching Civics and Current Events in the History Classroom, Grades 6-9
Sarah Cooper

Authentic Assessment in Social Studies: A Guide to Keeping It Real
David Sherrin

Facilitating Conversations About Race in the Classroom
Danielle Stewart, Martha Caldwell, Dietra Hawkins

Identity Affirming Classrooms: Spaces that Center Humanity
Erica Buchanan-Rivera

Teaching Towards Green Schools: Transforming K-12 Education through Sustainable Practices
Linda H. Plevyak

Learning to Depolarize

Helping Students and Teachers Reach Across Lines of Disagreement

Kent Lenci

Routledge
Taylor & Francis Group

NEW YORK AND LONDON

Designed cover image: Getty Images

First published 2023
by Routledge
605 Third Avenue, New York, NY 10158

and by Routledge
4 Park Square, Milton Park, Abingdon, Oxon, OX14 4RN

Routledge is an imprint of the Taylor & Francis Group, an informa business

© 2023 Kent Lenci

Library of Congress Cataloging-in-Publication Data
Names: Lenci, Kent, author.
Title: Learning to depolarize : helping students and teachers reach across lines of disagreement / Kent Lenci.
Description: New York, NY : Routledge, 2023. |
Series: Routledge eye on education |
Includes bibliographical references.
Identifiers: LCCN 2022019934 (print) | LCCN 2022019935 (ebook) |
ISBN 9781032266923 (hardback) | ISBN 9781032246604 (paperback) |
ISBN 9781003289494 (ebook)
Subjects: LCSH: Civics–Study and teaching–United States. |
Interpersonal communication–Study and teaching–United States. |
Social learning–United States. | Affective education–United States. |
Polarization (Social sciences)–United States. | United States–Politics and government–Study and teaching.
Classification: LCC LC1091 .L367 2023 (print) |
LCC LC1091 (ebook) | DDC 370.11/5–dc23/eng/20220803
LC record available at https://lccn.loc.gov/2022019934
LC ebook record available at https://lccn.loc.gov/2022019935

ISBN: 978-1-032-26692-3 (hbk)
ISBN: 978-1-032-24660-4 (pbk)
ISBN: 978-1-003-28949-4 (ebk)

DOI: 10.4324/9781003289494

Typeset in Palatino
by Newgen Publishing UK

Dedication

for my dad—
exemplary educator,
connoisseur of the written word,
and my biggest fan

Contents

Acknowledgments viii

Meet the Author xi

1   Introduction: We Have Always Been Those Students 1

2   Polarization Awaits Our Children 9

3   Depolarization Is a Job for Schools 21

4   Cross-Cutting Dialogue Through Cross-Country
    Connections 35

5   Teaching Students to Build Bridges Within the
    Classroom 50

6   Depolarization Requires Managing Media and
    Emotions 66

7   Positioning Faculty to Encourage Depolarization 87

8   Partnering With Parents Across the Political
    Divide 100

9   Conclusion: Finding the Courage to Depolarize 118

Appendix: Consolidated List of Resources 128

Works Cited 134

Acknowledgments

A number of former students and colleagues set me on the path to writing this book. I am indebted to the Brookwood employees (and one Brookwood parent) who volunteered to share their stories during our IDEA sessions; your courage enabled that gathering, and that gathering helped lay the groundwork for me to eventually write this book. To all of the Brookwood students who passed through seventh grade during the era of the Confederate flag partnership, I am also grateful. Some of you (if you ever happen to pick up this book) will find your insights and reactions in Chapter Four. I appreciate Stephanie Sefcik's partnership as I first launched that project and for introducing me to the battlefield in Franklin, TN. I am eternally grateful to Bo Garrett for his collaboration over the following years. For the purposes of this book, I thank Bo in particular for having shared his students' reactions to the word cloud (some of which appear in the manuscript) and for the use of that word cloud (I had to recreate it to meet the visual requirements of the publisher, but I think I got it right).

Thanks to Ben Wildrick, who, during a chance meeting in a parking lot, reminded me of the relevance of the work of Brookwood's science department, and thanks also to Annie Johnson for fleshing that out with me. Thanks to Sven Holch for sharing his current-events assignment, Bill Ivey for sharing his lesson on listening, and Karen Shorr for reminding me how this work connects to the learning of our youngest students. Charlotte Perrine, you will find yourself in this narrative if you look closely, and I thank you for letting me borrow an anecdote. I am grateful for Wolfgang Hoelscher's insight into the publishing world and Adam Kuhlmann's guidance as I took my first, tentative steps toward writing a book. And, at the risk of thanking Adam twice, I extend a special debt of gratitude to my former colleagues on Brookwood's Team Seven; you made it a pleasure to go to work!

Many people helped sharpen my ideas during the research phase of this project. I am grateful to Todd Rogers at Harvard's Kennedy School for his time and expertise and for introducing me to his colleague, Julia Minson, who was similarly helpful. Conversations with Caroline Blackwell, Vice President at NAIS, prompted me to think more deeply about the tension between supporting students of color and providing space for those whose opinions might cause them discomfort. Jennifer Cortez and Revida Rahman, founders of One WillCo, shared their efforts to support students of color in their local school system and introduced me to Lamont Turner, who appears in my narrative and to whom I am also grateful. Bonnie Snyder, Beth Feeley, and Ashley Jacobs each helped me extend my thinking after watching the Parents Unite conference, and I thank them for their time and insight.

A handful of authors deserve recognition. *Why We're Polarized*, by Ezra Klein, is an excellent book. Klein and I draw on the findings of many of the same researchers, and anyone looking for a more expansive discussion of polarization than I provide here should head straight to Klein. *The Political Classroom*, by Diana Hess and Paula McAvoy, is the go-to authority for high school teachers committed to the ideals of civic preparation. Finally, it would be difficult to overstate the influence of Arlie Russell Hochschild's *Strangers in Their Own Land* on my professional journey. Her book is a master class in empathy, and Hochschild embodies the aspirations I have for today's students as they face a polarized future.

A version of Chapter Seven first appeared as a series of three articles in Intrepid Ed News, and I thank Joel Backon for providing that platform.

I am grateful to my dad, who has always been my inspiration, and to Beverly, both of whom maintained interest in and support for this project from the first day to the last. I appreciate my children, Cooper and JD, who came home from school many days and asked hopefully, "Did you finish the book?" Finally, I am grateful for my wife, Jessica, who launched this project one day by saying simply, "You should write a book; that's what people do." She was right, as usual.

Meet the Author

For 20 years, Kent Lenci taught, coached, and occupied several leadership positions at the middle school level, first at Beaver Country Day School and more recently at Brookwood School. He is the recipient of various honors, including the Margot Stern Strom Teaching Award from Facing History and Ourselves and the Teacher of the Future designation from the National Association of Independent Schools. Kent has presented at local and national conferences, and his writing has appeared in a number of outlets, including Huff Post, Intrepid Ed, and Independent Teacher. He is a graduate of Friends School of Baltimore, Bucknell University, and the Harvard Graduate School of Education.

In 2019 Kent founded Middle Ground School Solutions, which is dedicated to helping schools honor political and ideological differences. Since then, he has delivered workshops to students and educators across a range of independent and public schools in the interest of easing the country's political polarization. His self-imposed exile from the daily life of schools is not likely to last all that long; he really misses teaching. Kent lives in Massachusetts with his wife and two children, Cooper and JD, where he spends much of his time on, in, or near the ocean. Kent can be reached through his website: www.middleground schools.com.

1

Introduction: We Have Always Been Those Students

For 20 years, like an undercover agent, I embedded myself among middle schoolers. Occasionally, I would emerge—to attend jury duty or renew my driver's license—and the escapes would leave me disoriented. People rode trains. They strolled. They occupied offices—*doing what?* They drank coffee, seemingly whenever the spirit moved them. They appeared oblivious to the structures that bound my day-to-day existence. *Is this what people do?* I would wonder. The world outside of school and the people who inhabited that world were remote and unfamiliar.

My domain was middle school, its schedule the rhythm of my life, its occupants the focus of my attention. These people could be awkward to the point of incapacitation, but they were endearing and funny. They were curious, and their energy was breathtaking. They were intensely social. They would save seats, crack jokes during class, and sometimes, like bull walruses, smash into each other in a feverish attempt to secure their slot in the social order. Their fortunes could change quickly. Monday morning might find them unaccountably excised from a previously secure group of friends, leaving them bewildered and bereft. To guard against such eventualities, they would lock arms as they marched down the hallway like a steamrolling wave of social security.

DOI: 10.4324/9781003289494-1

I learned many lessons during my two decades as a teacher: that I'd be sick by the second week of school (no pandemic required) and unavailable on weekends until mid-June; that taco Tuesdays were overrated but chocolate-milk Wednesdays worth the hype; that snow days still mattered. Above all else, despite my affection for them, I learned that middle schoolers were a different breed. It was not until I had taught these children for 20 years and coached 41 seasons of sports (including that one regrettable basketball season) that I realized, however, that I had been mistaken. In fact, the intense need for social affirmation and acceptance that defines middle school is not a stage through which one passes. It is not a skin to be shed on the way out of adolescence. It's training. We are the products of that training.

The Challenge of Political Polarization

We are also the victims of it. We have become a polarized society, bound unconditionally to those on our political team and mistrustful and dismissive of the others. We cling to our teammates, with whom we share a common cause, and we recoil from our opponents. We display tribal badges to advertise our allegiance, and we rage at the sight of our opponents' markings. The evidence of our polarization and the disfunction it causes is everywhere, so obvious now that it hardly merits explanation. How far back in time would we have to travel to unearth a more hopeful mindset? When in our history might we have assumed that a pandemic, a common enemy if there ever was one, could engender solidarity rather than enmity? How long have we been this polarized?

I am both optimistic and temperamentally moderate. I tend not to overreact. I'm primed to believe that polarization is cyclical, that this too shall pass. After all, we've seen division before. Preston Brooks beat Charles Sumner senseless right there on the floor of the Senate, for crying out loud! Even my seventh graders know that (although they also know the Civil War arrived shortly thereafter). I eased my way into the landscape of polarization from a place of caution and skepticism, alert for signs that this national "crisis" might not necessarily be all it's cracked up to be. I wondered if we might blame Donald Trump, the nation's most divisive president, in which case we might also infer that this polarization is fleeting. Alas, President Trump's polarizing effect—or his embodiment of our own polarization— affirms a trend that was already well in the works. This is not a passing phase.

The forces that drive our polarization are deep. Ancient threats conditioned humans to seek safety within the group and guard against danger from without. We are hardwired to crave group acceptance, and we are intrinsically inclined to view inter-group dynamics as a zero-sum game that we must win—or, just as compelling, that the other side must lose. Increasingly, the contest of politics has mapped onto that ancient blueprint for human behavior, and modern societal structures—most notably media—leverage that psychology to more deeply entrench us in a morass of division. It has become de rigueur for politicians to invite across-the-aisle cooperation, but no one really believes this political theater anymore. Our national condition, this debilitating polarization, is not mending, and we owe it to both our students and our society to address the crisis through education.

One could make a skills-based case for empowering students to reach across lines of ideological or political division. In a nation, as the author Bill Bishop put it, of "balkanized communities whose inhabitants find other Americans to be culturally incomprehensible,"[1] students will benefit from any training that helps them ford the divide. Will the kid from New England be willing to take that job down South some day? This depends how comfortable she would feel living among the "others" across the Mason-Dixon line. As with any other literacy, or a foreign language, it is reasonable to believe that students who have some facility for cross-cutting communication and collaboration will expand their otherwise narrowing options for employment, housing, and companionship.

Our students individually will require the skills and dispositions to help them reach across lines of political divide, but the plain, inescapable truth is that our country also requires this of them. As the nation absorbed the Capitol attack of January 2021, a Twitter post read, "Each person knocking down those doors once sat in a classroom."[2] There will always be conspiratorially minded people, and we will not eradicate extremism. But an attack on the seat of American government, perpetrated by Americans proudly waving American flags, reveals a societal disconnect so profound that it would be a dereliction of duty for educators to ignore the polarization that fueled it.

No sincere observer of our national condition could argue against the urgency of preparing tomorrow's citizens to pursue a more civil and productive path. And yet, it will not come naturally to educators to accept responsibility for helping to depolarize this country. To many teachers, schools occupy a place of intellectual purity, far from the dirty business of politics. In fact, though, we must divest ourselves of the delusion that schooling and politics are discrete realms. In many ways, the "political" is an inextricable feature of education—from the biases and assumptions carried by teachers, to the expectations and concerns of parents, to the content featured in a school's curriculum. Our use of language—and therefore our study of it—is political. History is political. Even science is political. This is a symbiotic relationship, a two-way street: our national discourse—politics—seeps into the life of the school, and learning informs our national discourse. For better and for worse, the state of our democracy tomorrow will reflect the education our students receive today.

In 2019 I left the classroom and, through my consulting business, began trying to help schools honor ideological and political differences. My first steps in this new realm were unsteady. Initially, I peddled myself as a first responder of sorts, tending to the political fires that flared up in schools—the student whose MAGA hat offended a classmate, or the faculty member whose activism was perceived as a form of indoctrination. There was a market for this, with school leaders feeling besieged by political pressures, particularly during electoral cycles. The discord bred of political matters was something to be managed, defended against. Politics was nothing but trouble, and schools wanted to keep trouble at bay—to soothe the aggrieved parent, to quiet the kerfuffle over the MAGA hat. Educators saw me as a partner in taming the storm.

Eventually, though, I got my story straight. I was not out to insulate schools from the divisiveness of politics. Instead, I wanted to prepare students to face that divisiveness. If anything, I was looking to start fires, not extinguish them. This book follows that modestly rebellious spirit. It is not a guide to managing political crises in schools. Rather, it contends that school life should prepare students to navigate—and hopefully mend— our political fractures and that, consequently, we must do all we can to deliver the skills required to productively engage in cross-cutting dialogue. We should be asking students to habitually engage with the "other," not trying to spare them (and us) the discord that comes from that engagement.

Chapters Two and Three, then, explain the causes and consequences of political polarization and contend that schools should shoulder some responsibility for depolarizing American society.

Meeting the Challenge in Schools

The remainder of the book describes how that might happen.

I taught social studies, which included explicitly political content: the workings of our federal government, the electoral process, current events. I was engrossed in civic education. But I do not project my particular classroom experience onto the reader. I maintain that politics and schooling are linked, yet the remedy for polarization will not be found exclusively in classrooms such as the one I occupied. A faded copy of the Constitution tacked to the bulletin board is not a prerequisite for playing a role in this work, and no single teacher or academic discipline should bear the responsibility for engendering curiosity about those with differing perspectives. This book is about building habits, not about implementing a single curriculum, and it serves a wide audience—not only of school leaders but also of teachers across grade levels and subject matters.

Diana Hess and Paula McAvoy already wrote an influential book called *The Political Classroom* that claims high-quality social studies instruction should include challenging, political discourse. I certainly agree, yet I also believe the story is much bigger than social studies. I suggest we bust down the classroom walls entirely by connecting our students with their counterparts in other schools to engage in cross-cutting dialogue, and I highlight the interplay of media literacy and social emotional learning (SEL) in our efforts to cultivate a generation of bridge-builders. Readers who embrace a collective responsibility for helping prepare our students to face a polarized society will find value in the book—not just the social studies teachers among us.

For several years, my Massachusetts students engaged in discussion and collaboration with their counterparts in the South. They entered those conversations burdened by stereotypes about the "other" across the Mason-Dixon line (as did their partners in Alabama), but familiarity softened the divide. That project helped me realize that, for students to navigate a politically polarized country, they need many opportunities to interact across lines of divide that we would not necessarily consider political. Chapter Four tells the tale of that cross-country collaboration.

Chapter Five contends that deliberative dialogue can be just as productive within a classroom as it can be across state lines. Most classrooms feature viewpoint diversity. To capitalize on that ideological diversity, we must establish norms of behavior that welcome, reward, and protect sincere and respectful exchanges across lines of disagreement, and we need to teach students the communication skills to bridge the gap with the political or ideological "other." Then we need to measure it. If we contend that thoughtful dialogue features painstaking, focused listening, for example, we need to start assessing the extent to which students practice such listening skills.

Chapter Six places social emotional intelligence at the core of a healthy approach to dialogue across lines of difference. Positive emotional responses bind us to our political team, just as negative emotions repel us from our political enemies and preempt productive, cross-cutting conversations. Social emotional learning therefore plays a central role in training the bridge-builders of tomorrow, and because emotion is fundamental to media's polarizing effect, the chapter simultaneously champions media literacy. So-called "fake news" has become alarmingly influential in shaping our collective perceptions of the "other," and the business model of modern news has deepened our divides. To face the unprecedented challenges of a fractured media landscape, our kids will need to develop a rigorous habit of critical inquiry. We adults have increasingly lost sight of our responsibilities as critical consumers of news, and kids need to reclaim them.

Chapter Seven asserts that we teachers need to do what we ask of our students. We must take stock of our media consumption to monitor bias. We should look to bridge-building organizations that leverage personal connection to ease political division, and schools should lead professional-development work that shines a light on our own polarization. We teachers cannot lead our students in a direction we have not, ourselves, at least attempted to travel.

We must also partner with the one constituency that holds the key to progress: parents. For many teachers, parents lurk in the shadows, ready to pounce when provoked by a controversial conversation or course of study. Conversely, many parents are filled with dread, worried about their children and uncertain whether school is a place to reinforce or undermine their family's values. If we are serious about preparing students to navigate a divided country, we need to open the lines of communication between school and parents when it comes to matters that either party would consider "political." This is the focus of Chapter Eight.

The book rests on a handful of interlocking assertions: that political polarization in this country presents a formidable and enduring challenge; that our polarization is rooted in social and emotional dynamics upon which education can shine a light; that this is our business—that we educators have a duty to ameliorate the situation by preparing students to reach across the political divide; and finally, that our students' success relies on our own willingness to engage in the introspection and outreach that will equip us to meet their needs.

Readers who are interested in exploring those claims will find the most value in this book. There is practical guidance to be found (proceed directly to Chapter Five for the most concentrated dose of it), but if this book makes a genuine contribution to the conversation, it will be in the provocation of new thinking and the application of extensive research from the social sciences to the life of the school. Educators know the business of school. Social scientists understand why we are polarized and what can be done about it. Here is a book to blend those two discrete realms.

We educators cannot continue to pretend that the polarized state of our democracy is not at least partially reflective of the education of its citizenry. Decades ago, the Supreme Court ruled that students do not shed their rights at the schoolhouse gates. Nor should we adults discard our civic responsibilities as we pass through those gates. The slogan of Friends School of Baltimore, from which I graduated, at one time read, "The world needs what our children can do." Our country, plagued by polarization, desperately needs what our children can do, if only we can find the courage and commitment to help them do it.

Notes

1   Bishop, 2008, p. 14
2   Nold, 2021

2

Polarization Awaits Our Children

On September 12, 2001, feeling wounded and heartbroken, I searched high and low for an American flag. The shelves were bare, though, and the moral psychologist Jonathan Haidt may well have been among the many Americans who beat me to the stores. In *The Righteous Mind*, he wrote, "It was as if there was an ancient alarm box in the back of my brain with a sign on it that said, 'In case of foreign attack, break glass and push button.' I hadn't known the alarm box was there, but when those four planes broke the glass and pushed the button I had an overwhelming sense of being American. I wanted to do something, anything, to support my team."[1]

Empty-handed still at the end of that disorienting week, I tied three strips of ribbon—red, white, and blue—to the antenna of my little sedan and drove from Massachusetts to suburban Washington, DC for a wedding. The northeast Route 95 corridor, normally ill-tempered, felt strangely hospitable. Motorists gave way to each other, and we slowed in unison while crossing the Hudson River, witnessing for ourselves the smoke still rising from the wreckage of Lower Manhattan. Months after that trip, the tattered ribbons remained on my antenna, a tangible reminder of my American identity.

DOI: 10.4324/9781003289494-2

The Power of Group Membership

Decades ago, Henri Tajfel and his colleagues showed that group membership profoundly influences human behavior.[2] They gathered together several dozen study participants and divided them into groups, ostensibly based on a quick showing of abstract paintings: those who preferred the paintings of Paul Klee, participants were told, were joined together, while those who favored Wassily Kandinsky were bundled separately. In fact, the groups were chosen randomly, leaving nothing more than the perception of a loosely shared aesthetic affinity to bind their members. As it turned out, even that tenuous bond was enough to trigger what Haidt has called "groupishness."[3] Granted the power to assign monetary rewards or penalties, the participants rewarded members of their own team and punished the others, working especially hard to maximize the profit margin of their squad over the opposition. Even if it meant a more meager payday for themselves, participants in the study laid down the hammer to ensure that as much difference as possible separated the winnings of the two arbitrarily formed groups. Tajfel and his co-authors summarized, "[I]t is the winning that seems more important to them."[4]

Almost every literary discussion of in-group favoritism or out-group punishment begins with Tajfel, so before I ever laid eyes on his study, I had come across many references to it. Those references, however, tended to omit a detail that, as a teacher, I found rather worth noting: the study's participants were 14- and 15-year-old boys. *Well of course they were trying to crush the other team*, I found myself thinking. *That's what eighth- and ninth-grade boys do! It doesn't take a world-renowned social psychologist to tell you that. Just put the kids on a playing field.*

Further digging, though, revealed that this innate disposition toward inter-group competition is not unique to the gender or age of Tajfel's study participants. It is not a phase through which adolescents pass. Humans are biologically programmed to see the world in groups—"hard-wired," as biologist and behavioral scientist Robert Sapolsky puts it, "for us/them dichotomies."[5] In the half century since Henri Tajfel presented his seminal study, a robust body of research has confirmed his findings. As the political scientist Shanto Iyengar and his colleagues note, "A vast literature in social psychology demonstrates that any such in-group/out-group distinction, even one based on the most trivial of characteristics, triggers both positive feelings for the in group and negative evaluations of the out group."[6]

That includes politics. For decades, the two main political parties in the United States have been sorting themselves into ever more distinct tribes, increasingly faithful in adopting stances in opposition to those of the other party (as Henri Tajfel might say, "It is the winning that seems more important"). Members of Congress have moved toward their parties' poles,[7] and gridlock reigns. Party allegiance within the public has reflected that purification. The Pew Research Center reports, "…[I]n 1994, 23% of Republicans were *more liberal* than the median Democrat; while 17% of Democrats were *more conservative* than the median Republican. Today, those numbers are just 1% and 3%, respectively."[8] As Ezra Klein points out in his book, *Why We're Polarized*, it was once common for people to "split the ticket" when voting—to cast a vote for a Republican candidate for president, for example, while voting Democratic for the local House seat—but by 2000, that practice had virtually evaporated.[9] Membership in the major political parties has become more crisply delineated, populated by people who increasingly think alike.

Ideological and Affective Polarization

Researchers call this type of polarization *ideological*. Within each party, there is increasing agreement about policy issues, while there is pointed disagreement with members of the opposing parties. Pew has tracked the trend. Are stricter environmental regulations worth the cost? In 1994, a similar share of Republicans and Democrats thought so. By 2017, in contrast, 77% of Democrats agreed with the statement, while only 36% of Republicans did.[10] In 1994, Democrats and Republicans disagreed as to whether racial discrimination impedes the success of African Americans—but not by much. By 2017, though, a huge gulf separated the perceptions of Democrats and Republicans on the issue of race.[11] On question after question—regarding regulation, gender, foreign policy, corporate responsibility, and many other topics—Republicans and Democrats increasingly disagree on the answers.[12]

We are polarized, however, by more than ideology. Regardless of what we think about *policies*, our perceptions of *each other* may be the more salient divider. Liliana Mason is among several prominent political scientists whose work explains the growing political divide. In *Uncivil Agreement: How Politics Became Our Identity*, Mason acknowledges the expanding ideological rift between Americans but adds, "A much larger division, however, is growing between them in their sense of themselves as liberals and conservatives. Democrats and Republicans have chosen ideological teams, and their sense of belonging to one side has divided them more powerfully than their policy differences have.... More than simply disagreeing, Democrats and Republicans are feeling like very different kinds of people."[13] This is known as *affective* polarization. Aside from any ideological differences that may divide us, we face a more daunting prospect: that we simply don't like each other.

Partisan antipathy is on the rise, with 81% of both Republicans and Democrats holding a negative view of the opposing party—up sharply from 1994.[14] As Shanto Iyengar and his colleagues write, "Democrats and Republicans both say the other party's members are hypocritical, selfish, and close-minded, and they are unwilling to socialize across party lines, or even to partner with opponents in a variety of other activities."[15] According to Pew, partisanship has become more divisive than even race or ethnicity.[16]

That animosity affects our behavior. According to Iyengar and Sean Westwood, people no longer even hide their disdain for the political other.[17] Pulling from a wide range of research for their 2019 article, "The Origins and Consequences of Affective Polarization in the United States," Iyengar, Westwood, and colleagues show how our politics has impacted seemingly non-political behavior.[18] One study found employers more likely to pursue candidates whose resumes indicated shared political leanings,[19] and another suggested that people would weigh political party over grade point average when deciding who should receive a college scholarship.[20] Liliana Mason's research has shown evidence of partisan bias in both grading and college admissions.[21]

We discriminate against the political other, and we increasingly stick to our own political tribe. We have few friends across the aisle,[22] and we shy away from forging new relationships with those people. Gregory Huber and Neil Malhotra analyzed data from online dating platforms to reveal that people favor those who are ideologically similar when seeking a long-term partner,[23] and Liliana Mason has found that political partisans prefer not to mix with the political others.[24] In 2008, Bill Bishop wrote *The Big Sort* to catalogue all the ways in which Americans have increasingly clustered themselves with like-minded compatriots. He wrote, "Party membership is not simply an affiliation. It's a screen that filters and shapes the way we perceive the world."[25] We have increasingly divided that world into those we trust and those we do not.

Anything for the Team

Our allegiance to political party is in fact threatening to undermine our individual agency. We seek the wisdom of our political compatriots even when confronted with good reasons *not* to trust those people on certain matters,[26] and we elevate our group identity above our individual policy preferences. In 2003, Geoffrey Cohen showed that partisan identity exerts a greater pull than ideology. He gathered an ideologically diverse sampling of college students and asked them to judge two versions of a welfare proposal. One provided generous benefits, while the other was more austere. For some study participants, Cohen labeled the proposals as if they had been supported by an overwhelming majority of either House Democrats or Republicans.

The results of the study were stark: objective evaluation seemed to evaporate in the presence of party imprimatur. "For both liberal and conservative students, the effect of reference group information overrode that of policy content. If their party supported it, liberals supported even a harsh welfare program, and conservatives supported even a lavish one."[27] In other words, the study participants followed the herd. Professing to stand for liberal or conservative ideals was no barrier to supporting policies in conflict with those ideals. Interestingly, people denied that their judgements were based on anything other than a fair, objective reading of the proposals; politics, they insisted, had nothing to do with it.

A recent study affirmed Cohen's discovery that group identity can subjugate an individual's policy preferences. Michael Barber and Jeremy Pope seized what they considered a novel opening in American politics: the chance to study the effect of a party leader—President Trump—whose public statements demonstrated an unusual degree of ideological fluidity. In the face of that fluidity, the researchers sought to track whether people stuck to their ideological guns if their positions were challenged by the party leader. "The very nature of Trump's non-ideological and ever-changing issue positions is what allows us the unique opportunity to identify moments when issue content and party are in conflict," they wrote. "And this divergence allows us to identify which of these attachments appears to be more important in the minds of the typical voter."[28] In other words, they wondered whether Cohen had been correct in determining that party affiliation outweighs an individual's policy preferences. Would those who identified themselves as deeply conservative maintain their principles in the face of mixed messaging from the president? Or, if forced to choose, would their allegiance to party overcome their ideological purity?

The researchers chose ten issues on which President Trump had publicly offered conflicting positions, and they asked study participants, given a cue from the president, to indicate their level of support for each matter. One group was asked, for example, whether they supported or opposed raising the minimum wage above $10 an hour, with the following qualifier: "Donald Trump has said he supports this policy. What about you?"[29] Another group of respondents was asked a similar question, but with the wording changed to say that Trump had opposed the policy (which he had).

As expected, Barber and Pope found that Republicans followed their leader: when told that Trump had supported a policy—whether or not it was ideologically liberal or conservative—Republicans tended to indicate support for it. Interestingly, those who identified themselves as strong conservatives were most strongly influenced by Trump's lead—no matter the ideological direction he took. "In other words, partisan identity is so powerful that a respondent's self-labelled ideology is often at odds with their expressed policy positions when given cues from a party leader."[30] Barber and Pope concluded their study by observing that polarization is at its essence a matter of belonging. "It has much more to do with partisan loyalty than it does with ideological principal."[31] Liliana Mason's research leads her to the same conclusion. Despite the popular perception that people choose political parties as a reasoned process of supporting the political team that most accurately reflects one's policy preferences, in fact it is the opposite: people alter their policy preferences to align with political-party affiliation.[32]

Decades ago, Henri Tajfel documented the power of group membership, and today we see that dynamic reflected in our political loyalties. We mistrust, avoid, and discriminate against the political other, while seeking the embrace of our political brethren. Our identity, increasingly, is attached to our politics, and our sense of belonging within the political tribe is even powerful enough to suppress our individual policy preferences. In short, who we are as individuals is increasingly tied to who we are as members of the political group.

According to Liliana Mason, our allegiance to that political tribe is amplified by the convergence of what used to be fractured elements of our social identities. Our inclination toward what Haidt called "groupishness" used to be tempered by the multiplicity of our identities. We were Republicans, perhaps, but we were also Catholics, let's say, and middle class. Each of these distinct identities helped dilute the pull of the others. Increasingly, though, says Mason, those formerly distinct social identities have begun to align themselves with political-party identification.

"The American political parties are growing socially polarized. Religion and race, as well as class, geography, and culture, are dividing the parties in such a way that the effect of party identity is magnified. The competition is no longer between only Democrats and Republicans."[33] Instead, it feels as if the competition is being waged between two distinct tribes, which are themselves bolstered by other, complementary social identities. And as these formerly distinct identities layer themselves on top of each other, a threat to one triggers a defense of all. Politics has become something of a shorthand for the great cultural battle between two warring American camps.

Our Polarization Is Chronic

My research for this project revealed one recurring glimmer of hope—that a superordinate goal might someday provide a tonic to soothe our divide.[34] Perhaps, went the thinking, we Americans might eventually identify a challenge—a pandemic, for example—so incontrovertibly formidable that it would be unavoidably unifying—that we might get out of our own way and band together in common cause. In 2019, the Nuclear Threat Initiative and Johns Hopkins University issued a report called the "Global Health Security Index," assessing the world's preparedness for transnational disease outbreaks. While no country fared particularly well in the analysis, the United States came out on top. Out of all 195 countries surveyed, the United States was deemed the best positioned to avoid and respond to a pandemic.[35]

In hindsight, that relative optimism—the reminder of how things might have gone—feels like a punch in the gut. By objective measures, the United States has not weathered the pandemic well.[36] The very sort of challenge that many thought could be a unifying force for solidarity in fact intensified the country's bitter divisions, with the public's response to masking and vaccines sharpening our predictable battle lines. The Global Health Security Index was a measure of scientific and structural preparedness. It failed to account for the ways that polarization would undermine the nation's response. According to a Pew survey, Americans resoundingly say the country has become more divided since the outbreak of the pandemic.[37] We agree, at least, on that much.

I entered into my research for this writing project concerned by our national polarization and convinced we needed to do something about it. Polarization felt acute, like a searing pain, with the evidence of our national ailment seemingly everywhere. The country had recently weathered two presidential impeachments, the acrimonious, deeply contested presidential election of 2020 and the 2021 attack on the nation's Capitol. There seemed to be little to unify anyone about anything—except possibly the shared understanding that we Americans could agree on nothing. As acute as the crisis of polarization had felt, though, I had to assume that we are living in uniquely divisive times— that it hasn't always been this way and that, perhaps, it won't stay this way.

As I read, though, I found myself surprised by the extent to which this condition was, in fact, chronic. If it appears that our polarization cannot get much worse, it is also true that writers have been expressing this sentiment for years. In 2018, the publication of Senator Ben Sasse's book *Them: Why We Hate Each Other and How to Heal* spoke to a debilitating estrangement among the American electorate. A decade earlier, President Barrack Obama had come to office promising to ease the toxic polarization of American politics.[38] And writing about the landscape before Obama's tenure, Bill Bishop wrote, "Although the two parties emerged from the 2006 midterm elections as polarized as at any time since the end of World War Two, this kind of polarization can't last."[39] It has not only lasted, it has intensified. President George W. Bush was the most polarizing president in modern history until President Obama took office, and his divisiveness was then eclipsed by President Trump.[40]

The fracture has increasingly assumed sinister overtones. During the summer of 2021, Democrats and Republicans sparred over their vision for a new infrastructure bill. Democrats sold the bill as a common-sense prescription to address long-deferred upgrades to the nation's infrastructure, while Republicans opposed the expense and broad reach of the legislation. In that

sense, the tussle maintained the tradition of ideological opposition that has existed for decades in American politics. In August,
the bill passed the Senate, and in November, with the support of
13 Republicans, it cleared the House.

Several of those Republicans then received death threats,
highlighting the extraordinary antipathy that defines today's political polarization. One caller hoped Representative Don Bacon
would fall down a staircase.[41] A New York man was arrested for
threatening Representative Andrew Garbarino.[42] Representative
Fred Upton's office received an expletive-laden phone call
expressing the hope that he, his staff, and his family would all
perish. The caller called Upton a "traitor," language that echoes
Representative Marjorie Taylor Greene who, as the vote loomed,
had declared that any Republican voting for the bill should be
considered "a traitor to our party, a traitor to their voters and a
traitor to our donors."[43]

Representative Adam Kinzinger, advised by a caller to "slit
his wrists" after the infrastructure vote,[44] had, months earlier,
received an outraged letter from family members disgusted by
his criticism of President Trump. "Oh my," the letter begins,
"what a disappointment you are to us and to God! We were
once so proud of your accomplishments! Instead, you go against
your principles and join the 'devil's army' (Democrats and the
fake news media)."[45] It would be easy to dismiss the letter as
an unhinged outburst from the margins of Kinzinger's personal
life, were it not so consonant with the acrimonious tenor of tribal
warfare that has come to characterize American civic engagement; that letter's message of betrayal speaks to the broader
tenor of American society. Just as I once felt my American identity attacked by four hijacked planes, so too do many Americans
feel that their identity is under constant threat by the political
"other." You are with us, or you are against us, a loyal member
of the tribe or, in the words of Kinzinger's relatives, a soldier in
the "devil's army."

This debilitating polarization is not a painful flare-up. It is,
increasingly, our national reality, bemoaned and documented for
years now, and it would be a delusion to write off this condition as a passing trend. As Pew notes, the United States is unique

in its polarization—"exceptional," as they put it, "in its political divide."[46]

Conclusion: This Polarization Cannot Be Ignored

This, then, is the country into which we will send today's students: a nation at odds ideologically, one in which gridlock defines government and disagreement over every major policy question cleaves the electorate. We are a nation of human beings, and human nature leads us to seek the protection of the in-group and mistrust the out-group. That psychological instinct has increasingly manifested itself in a national sense of "us" and "them." We don't just disagree on the issues; we feel antipathy toward those who occupy the groups associated with those issues. A school that takes seriously its mandate to prepare students for the world that awaits them simply cannot ignore this polarization.

Notes

1 Haidt, 2012, p. 189
2 Tajfel et al., 1971
3 Haidt, 2012, p. 218
4 Tajfel et al., 1971, p. 172
5 Jacobs, 2018
6 Iyengar et al., 2019, p. 130
7 Abramowitz & Saunders, 2008
8 Pew Research Center, 2017 "The Partisan Divide…"
9 Klein, 2020, p. 8
10 Pew Research Center, 2017 "Global Warming…"
11 Pew Research Center, 2017 "The Partisan Divide…"
12 Pew Research Center, 2017 "The Partisan Divide…"
13 Mason, 2018, p. 29
14 Pew Research Center, 2017 "Partisan animosity…"
15 Iyengar et al., 2019, p. 130
16 Pew Research Center, 2019
17 Iyengar & Westwood, 2015

18   Iyengar et al., 2019
19   Gift & Gift, 2015
20   Iyengar & Westwood, 2015
21   Mason, 2018, p. 50
22   Pew Research Center, 2017 "Partisan animosity…"
23   Huber & Malhotra, 2017
24   Mason, 2018, p. 55
25   Bishop, 2008, p. 231
26   Marks et al., 2019
27   Cohen, 2003, p. 811
28   Barber & Pope, 2019, p. 11
29   Barber & Pope, 2019, p. 10
30   Barber & Pope, 2019, p. 4
31   Barber & Pope, 2019, p. 27
32   Mason, 2018, p. 21
33   Mason, 2018, p. 14
34   Mason, 2018, p. 134
35   Nuclear Threat Initiative, 2019
36   Bremmer, 2020; Chang, et al., 2022
37   Mordecai & Connaughton, 2020
38   Galston, 2010
39   Bishop, 2008, p. 298
40   Dunn, 2020
41   Edmonson, 2021
42   Associated Press, 2021
43   Sonmez, 2021
44   Edmonson, 2021
45   Read the Document, 2021
46   Dimock & Wike, 2020

3

Depolarization Is a Job for Schools

But do schools have a responsibility to help depolarize the country? The conventional wisdom is to steer well clear of politics. In 2020, I led a workshop with middle school students that was to serve as a deep dive into the Constitution. In the final run-up to the workshop, I received several anxious emails asking that I avoid mentioning any particular politician. The school looked forward to my lesson on the first article of the Constitution, but there would be no need to name names. The message in being invited to teach about the presidency without naming President Trump—the same message I have consistently encountered in my 20 years in schools—was clear: we don't get into politics.

It's Not Enough to Know… or Even to Think

School leaders may in fact agree that polarization is a national crisis but at the same time feel that the purity of schooling does not permit the intrusion of politics. In that case, their consciences may be somewhat soothed by the promise of education generally to engender a more functional citizenry—without wading into the mess of politics, specifically. If the problem is that we Americans can agree on nothing, perhaps with a deeper pool of shared, common knowledge, we may make progress. Or at least one might assume so.

DOI: 10.4324/9781003289494-3

The topic of climate change helps us see the limitations of this assumption; knowing more does not necessarily defuse polarization. Once upon a time, global warming—like many issues—was less politically divisive than it has become. In 1988, Vice President George H. W. Bush committed to environmental stewardship during his presidential campaign,[1] and a decade later a similar share of Republicans and Democrats believed that climate change had already arrived.[2] Soon, though, any common ground on this issue began to erode. Interviews with former members of Congress reveal that, as climate change became identified with the activism of Al Gore and, by extension, the Democratic party, it was untenable for Republicans to associate themselves with the cause. Former senator, Tim Wirth, in characterizing Republicans' mindset at the time, said, "If you are interested in climate change, that means you're supporting Al Gore."[3]

Today, any political accord on the issue of climate change seems laughable. It is "the toughest, most intractable political issue we, as a society, have ever faced," according to the Brookings Institute.[4] About 80% of liberal Democrats believe the Earth's warming is due to human activity, while only 15% of conservative Republicans agree.[5] "Across the board," says the Pew Research Center, "from possible causes to who should be the one to sort this all out, liberal Democrats and conservative Republicans see climate-related matters through vastly different lenses."[6]

Many of the issues that cleave our society have no "wrong answer," as we teachers like to say. Reasonable people marshal informed arguments regarding moral or philosophical disagreements: the collective right of a society to live peaceably versus the constitutional right to bear arms, for example. Yet on the matter of climate change, there is in fact a correct answer: the Earth is warming dangerously, and we humans are to blame. The issue is a matter of fierce political dispute in the United States, yet human-induced climate change is simply a fact, supported by an overwhelming body of empirical evidence.[7] That this is the case would suggest that science should bridge the political divide. Education must be the answer.

In fact, though, it may not be. Dan Kahan, a Yale professor of both law and psychology, studies what he calls the "science-of-science-communication"—or the way that scientific knowledge is communicated to and understood by the public. In particular, Kahan has devoted considerable professional attention to the issue of climate change, and his findings may vex those of us in schools who presume that, when people learn stuff, problems get solved.

According to Kahan, studies show no meaningful correlation between a person's scientific savvy and his or her belief in human-caused climate change (a conclusion reached by Pew, as well[8]). That's right: knowing more about science does not make a person more inclined to believe that humans are causing the Earth to heat up. Rather, Kahan has discovered that increasing scientific literacy goes hand in hand with political polarization on the issue of climate change.[9] In a 2015 study, Kahan found that, among liberal Democrats, increasing scientific literacy corresponded to a more fervent belief in human-induced climate change; the more a liberal Democrat knows about the science, the more he or she is convinced of the problem of climate change. In contrast, among conservative Republicans, the effect is inverted: increasing scientific literacy leads to a slightly *decreasing* tendency to declare that global warming is caused by humans. Kahan's findings appear paradoxical—how could knowing more about science possibly lead someone to doubt the urgency of climate change?—but only if one sees this as a question of scientific understanding. The issue, in fact, is not knowledge. It's identity.

Common sense suggests that we look out for ourselves, and psychologists report that our sense of identity exists at the core of what we consider the self. When our identity is threatened, we protect it, which can include what is known as "identity-protective reasoning"—attending to and interpreting information in a way that affirms our self-image while discarding or discrediting information that challenges our perception of the self.[10] For many liberals, science bolsters the feeling of solidarity with the political tribe. Apoplexy about the climate crisis is a visible badge of membership among progressives, and the science, while unsettling, affirms the tribal identity; it is, in that perverse sense, welcome. To be a card-carrying conservative these days, though, is to be among a cohort whose identity has been sharpened in opposition to the radical climate activists, and scientific proof of climate change is therefore, one might say, an "inconvenient truth."

Psychologically, the empirical evidence of climate change is a threat to the identity of some conservatives, because it is received as a threat to the group: *you are a bunch of science deniers.* Allegiance to the climate-denial camp—even in the face of conflicting scientific evidence—reflects a rational decision to conform to the norms of the in-group—to fit in. "[I]ndividuals," says Kahan, "predictably attend to information as identity-protective reasoners because of the greater impact that their personal actions and words have on their group status than they do on the risks that they or anyone else faces."[11] In other words, it's entirely possible that a person can both understand the science and, at the same time, toe the conservative line on climate change, because the long-term danger posed to a single person by the effects of climate change appears less consequential than the prospect of being cast out of the group. Remember, those students clinging to each other in our schools' hallways are learning to be *us*—members of social groups whose intrinsic need for belonging can override the rational side of our thought processes.

And that includes liberals, whose support of climate-change policies diminishes when they associate those policies with the political opposition. In a recent study, Leaf Van Boven, Phillip Ehret, and David Sherman presented participants with two possible approaches to limiting carbon pollution—a cap-and-trade system and a carbon tax. Democrats strongly supported each system when led to believe the policies originated within their party. When told the policies had been created by Republicans, though, their support waned considerably. Republicans demonstrated a similar pattern, scaling back their support of either policy if it was labeled as a Democratic idea. "Political polarization over climate policy does not simply reflect that Democrats and Republicans disagree about climate change," the researchers wrote, "but that Democrats and Republicans disagree with each other."[12] As Geoffrey Cohen has also shown, we are inclined to support measures associated with our group—whether or not those measures reflect what we say is important to us.

To summarize: climate change is a matter of settled science, yet the understanding of science does not lead to accord on the issue. For liberals, knowing more about science correlates with a commitment to the cause: climate change is a real problem. For conservatives, though, knowing more about science actually leads to voicing a deeper skepticism about climate change. This effect can be explained by our tendency as humans to attend to information that reinforces our identity and to deflect information that challenges that identity. Because our identities are increasingly intertwined with political tribes, we adopt the party line: conservatives demonstrate their loyalty by faithfully opposing the radical climate activists who are hellbent on undermining the American way of life, while liberals support a carbon tax to ease the existential climate crisis—unless they are told it's a Republican idea, in which case their support wilts.

The lesson for us educators is that solving the complex problems facing our society will require more than knowledge. It's just not enough to know things. Decades of work in the field of education have warned against the inadequacy of filling students like empty vessels or depositing information into them as if they were banks,[13] and many of us, knowing that facts alone do not constitute an education, have spent our careers trying to teach students to think critically about their worlds. This is certainly true of me, and it is true of the schools in which I have worked and, more broadly, the educational networks in which those schools exist.

If I were to choose a single mantra to represent my professional experience, it would be, "We teach kids how to think." For me, that goal has always assumed a certain purity in careful thinking—that rigorous, rational, reasoned consideration delivers an agreed-upon truth. For years, I stood in front of seventh graders and, feeling clever, argued both sides of a free-speech case to grease the wheels of critical thinking. I required students to defend theses in writing. I did all the things responsible history teachers do to get their kids to think, and I suppose I harbored an assumption that these mental calisthenics were shaping up my students for civic engagement. But research has shown me the limits of this assumption.

I am not so jaded as to believe that we have entered a "post-truth" world, as some have suggested. Even with Siri on call and artificial intelligence promising to relieve us entirely of the burden of thought someday, information is still undeniably helpful and, of course, we will keep teaching it in schools. But we cannot delude ourselves into thinking that a shared pool of common knowledge will turn the students of today into the bridge-builders of tomorrow. It is insufficient to believe in the unifying power of reason, because we humans have a tendency to deflect rational arguments that challenge our identities. Based on the research into the polarization of climate change, it is reasonable to infer that, when it comes to other, similarly contentious topics, the pull of group affiliation is powerful enough to sometimes muscle out a consideration of objective knowledge. That should suggest to us that education, as it has before, must evolve to meet the needs of today.

Will Civic Education Lead to Depolarization?

For many, that evolution includes an emphasis on civics. If the American political system is in crisis, then it reasonably follows that we should brush up on our understanding of that system. There is general agreement that such a refresher is long overdue. A 2017 report by the National Conference of State Legislatures indicated that a mere 30% of students in grades four, eight, and twelve were proficient in civics,[14] and the 2016 report "A Crisis in Civic Education" revealed that college students don't fare a whole lot better. Many of them lack basic constitutional knowledge—such as being able to identify which branch of American government has the power to declare war.[15] Only a third of native-born Americans can pass the test that stands between immigrants and their American citizenship.[16] Predictably, the lamentable state of civics awareness has spurred calls for action. Several years ago, the National Council for the Social Studies (NCSS) made the case for "Revitalizing Civic Education in Our Schools,"[17] and a flurry of state legislatures have recently considered civic-education bills.[18]

I can certainly appreciate the call for civics education, having spent the better part of 20 years trying to deliver it. I was the guy with the American flag tie around my neck and the Declaration of Independence on my bulletin board. I was the teacher handing out pocket Constitutions and, to the delight of some students and the embarrassment of others, acting out what I would do if a mugger ordered me to recite the First Amendment. A T-shirt hung on my wall featuring a man with exceptionally hairy arms under the header, "The Right to Bear Arms." So, it probably makes sense that, in the fall of 2016, I was the one leading students through an electoral activity in the name of civics education that only later did I decide may not have been the greatest idea.

The Sorting Hat: Assigning Students to Their Political Tribe

The 2016 presidential election approached my progressive New England school like a distant hurricane—menacing at first but then, as the forecasters gained confidence in Hillary Clinton's impending win, rather exciting. By the time the storm was imminent, it felt more like an opportunity to go down to the beach and watch the big waves than any sort of genuine hazard. My job, I felt, was simply to harness the power of all that energy surging up the coast and use it to draw students into the awesome swirl of electoral politics.

It is a cliché for teachers to try to "bring their subject to life," but, cliché or not, I was faithful to that goal. I had been bored enough as a history student and I dreaded inflicting that boredom on another generation. During our study of the Bill of Rights, I would line up my students and inform them gravely that due to recent, unmentionable events I would need to examine their text messages. When their hearts recovered, they found themselves interested in the right to privacy promised by the Fourth Amendment. This was my modus operandi—find a hook and leverage it to administer some learning. As the presidential election of 2016 drew near, I cast about for those hooks. We called the White House. We launched a contest to predict the Electoral College vote. But the activity that really lit kids up was the online quiz matching them with their political soulmate.

A handful of online tools will get this job done. One quiz asks a series of policy-related questions and then labels the user with a political typology (core conservative, solid liberal, etc.),[19] while another, after a similar question-and-answer regime, matches the user with the political party or candidate most closely aligned with his or her ideology.[20] As far as hooks go, I expected this one to be only moderately effective, but it turned out to be surprisingly alluring to my students. Armed with laptops and bright eyes, students engaged each other in discussion, compared notes, and plunged ever deeper into the online question-and-answer until, one by one, they were paired with their matching candidate or political typology. I could practically see the wheels of democratic engagement spring to life.

Engagement is a principal objective of civics education. The National Council for the Social Studies describes the goal of schooling as arming students with "the knowledge, skills, and dispositions needed for active and engaged civic life,"[21] which echoes the wording of the Center for American Progress: "When civics education is taught effectively, it can equip students with the knowledge, skills, and disposition necessary to become informed and engaged citizens."[22] If this is the goal of civics education—to become an engaged citizen—my electoral activity that day was a win. Students were finding their place in the political landscape by starting to think of themselves as "Clinton supporters" or, perhaps (more rarely in my Massachusetts classroom), "core conservatives." They were sketching themselves into the portrait of American democracy.

In the process, they were also joining teams. As each student found their way to the end of their questions, they moved themselves around the room to join others who had the same results. For many students, the revelation of "their" political party or "their" candidate was visibly reassuring—as if the sorting hat had just named the correct Hogwarts house. The PBS article touting one of these quizzes reads, "Take the political party quiz to find out where you fit!"[23] At a stage when kids are particularly anxious to know just that—where they fit—I opened the door to our national divide and put them right in their places.

For children, political-party membership can seem pretty concrete. Many seventh graders I've taught don't understand why a Democrat would ever wear a red tie, since it appears to violate the partisan dress code. A sixth grader I spoke to was surprised to learn that party affiliation can be changed, and a third grader didn't know you were allowed to befriend someone outside your political party. Party membership appears permanent and immutable to children. It is not, yet kids may be closer to the truth than we would like to imagine. According to Shanto Iyengar and colleagues, party membership is a particularly strong marker of identity, in part because it develops early in life.[24] Jonathan Haidt writes, "People bind themselves into political teams that share moral narratives. Once they accept a particular narrative, they become blind to alternative moral worlds."[25] Political allegiance may not be quite as black and white as children imagine, but given what we know about group psychology, it is a more powerful force than we'd like to admit. My political-typology lesson certainly engaged students, but it may have simultaneously kick-started their introduction to polarization.

There is a natural, perhaps unspoken, assumption in American society that civic "engagement" is an unquestionably elevated state of democratic being that encompasses everything we want in a citizen. On one hand, that would include the reasoned, measured, and thoughtful dialogue of an open-minded citizen who contributes productively to the national discourse and whose curiosity leaves room for personal growth and transformation; this is the image of deliberative democracy. Civic engagement also evokes the initiative and spark and commitment of the person whose activism—through voting or other measures—moves the civic agenda; this is participatory democracy.

In her book, *Hearing the Other Side*, political scientist Diana Mutz discusses the tension between these two elements of democracy—participatory and deliberative. She points out that deliberation is not necessarily conducive to participation. In fact, she says, the recipe for a high degree of democratic participation includes homogeneity of thought. "Like-minded people," she says, "can spur one another on to collective action and promote the kind of passion and enthusiasm that are central to motivating political participation."[26] That political participation is also stoked by animosity toward those across the aisle.[27]

In *The Political Classroom*, Diana Hess and Paula McAvoy show that students hailing from what they call "Like-Minded Schools (LMS)"—that is, schools with little political diversity— are a politically engaged group. "In short," they write, "these students are growing up being groomed for democratic participation—though much of it involves engaging in discussions with people who are ideologically alike."[28] In follow-up surveys, Hess and McAvoy found that these students were far more likely to vote than other students. They were also more politically partisan. Mutz, as well as Hess and McAvoy, makes clear that in fact it is the *lack* of deliberation—the formation of tight-knit communities of likeminded people—that inspires the greatest political participation.

Unfortunately, researchers report that it is these very people—righteous, active citizens—who, fortified by the agreeable support of their like-minded cohort, repel those across the aisle. A recent paper by James Druckman and colleagues examines the phenomenon of "mis-estimating affective polarization"—in which the degree of animus toward the political "other" can be explained in part due to a tendency to overgeneralize. People picture the most extreme example of the out-group and generalize that across the entirety of the tribe, leaving them feeling repelled by the entire lot. Druckman et al. observe the irony in referring to these animated, engaged, politically savvy citizens as "ideal voters." In fact, they say, it is those people who are turning off their counterparts across the political aisle. They write, "Our results suggest that these idealized citizens provoke animosity and hence fuel affective polarization. Not only that, these citizens often are the ones harboring the most animosity."[29] In short, there is evidence to suggest, regrettably, that political engagement exacerbates polarization.

Hence my ambivalence when I recall that electoral exercise in 2016. While I am not so vain as to believe that any single class-room activity did all that much lasting harm or good for my students, I now realize that I had fallen into a somewhat lazy assumption—that in grabbing the attention and interest of my students, I would set them on a path to democratic engagement that would encompass both participation and deliberation. These students were obviously discovering the intrigue of elect-oral politics, but in starting to see themselves as "Democrats" or "Republicans," they were also entering the first stage of our national, tribal conflict. We humans are intrinsically inclined to seek safety in the tribe, and modern forces have driven our tribes farther and farther apart. Political identity already is thrust upon us early in life, and once we bind ourselves to a pol-itical team, we are blind to alternate perspectives. The last thing we need is to be accelerating that process, and yet, in employing those quizzes, I probably did just that. All of which is to say, just as it is inadequate to assume that education generally is a ticket to depolarization, "civic education" more specifically may fall short.

Or maybe not. It depends, perhaps, on what we mean by the term "civic education." Most descriptions of civic education lead with the participatory element of the democratic ideal—the "active and engaged" language of the NCSS[30] and the "engaged citizen" reference from the Center for American Progress.[31] An influential report called "The Civic Mission of Schools" says civic education should lead people to "participate in their communi-ties" and "act politically."[32] When organizations present metrics to measure the success of civic education, they often include participatory markers—such as the rate at which people vote.[33] Various organizations include some reference to deliberation, but it's never the lead.

This book seeks to elevate the deliberative element of dem-ocracy to the headline: for today's students to successfully navigate—and possibly mend—our deeply polarized society, they must get better at productively interacting with the political and ideological "other" than we adults are currently doing.

Conclusion: School-Based Prevention, Not Lab-Based Intervention

American society is deeply polarized. An educator who agrees with that statement might then logically infer that education generally could ease that disfunction—that a more knowledgeable citizenry will grow into a more productive, cohesive cohort. After all, as the Schoolhouse Rock theme song used to remind me each and every Saturday morning, "knowledge is power!"

It is sobering, though, to acknowledge the limits of that power and to accept that education is in fact associated with polarization. Alan Abramowitz and Kyle Saunders have shown that ideological polarization is higher among those with more education,[34] and Diana Mutz has found that people with graduate degrees engage in the least amount of cross-cutting dialogue; those who have not finished high school engage in the most.[35] This finding may help explain why Democrats who did not graduate from high school are three times more accurate than those with postdoctorate degrees when asked to imagine how Republicans feel about contentious issues.[36] A 2019 study also found that the most politically intolerant Americans are the best educated.[37]

We now know that knowledge may indeed be powerful, but it alone is not enough to grease the wheels of deliberative democracy. I taught for 20 years. I believe in the power of education. But I sound a cautionary note that the mere dissemination of information—and even the encouragement of "critical thinking"—will do little to ease the crisis of polarization. Research has shown us that the pull of group membership—and the push of out-group animus—is also powerful.

If education generally may not meet the moment, civic education holds allure for many people. The pocket Constitution that I used to brandish in front of middle schoolers still sits on my home desk. I will always champion the teaching of our democratic system, and I am convinced that participation in our democratic machinery is a good thing. Still, I respect the researchers who help us see that fervent participation is associated with increased polarization. We must elevate the importance of deliberative democracy—of engaging respectfully and productively even across lines of difference and disagreement. I gently add my voice to the chorus of those calling for renewed attention to civic education—while emphasizing that such attention must include the deliberative element of democracy.

One of the many resources I consulted while researching this book was a social psychologist who explores interventions that help people communicate across lines of disagreement. She made a quick reference to a large undertaking in which researchers brought people together from across the country for a weekend of cross-cutting political conversation that yielded promising results; by following the researchers' protocols, folks broke down some political barriers.[38] In passing, this social psychologist mentioned that, given an entire weekend, she too could probably "move the needle" by applying an intervention that helped soften the lines of political divide. Alas, she told me, most lab research involves shorter experiments.

I found myself thinking that the political scientists and social psychologists whose insights and studies inform this book are missing an extraordinary opportunity. A weekend? How about 13 or 14 years? Why, as we face the enormity of this crisis, would we try to help those who are already the most polarized become slightly less so, without turning wholeheartedly to the nation's future citizenry, the voters-to-be, the consumers and creators of tomorrow's media? Why would we not attend to the humans whose minds we know to be the most elastic, the ones who are, by their very nature, most amenable to an unwritten script?

The following chapters sketch the contours of such an intervention—or rather, a possible approach to *prevention* of toxic polarization.

Notes

1   Worland, 2017
2   Kamarck, 2019
3   Van Boven et al., 2018, p. 497
4   Kamarck, 2019

5   Pew Research Center, 2016 "Politics of Climate"
6   Pew Research Center, 2016 "Politics of Climate"
7   Intergovernmental Panel on Climate Change
8   Pew Research Center, 2016 "Public knowledge about science…"
9   Kahan, 2015
10 Kaplan et al., 2016
11 Kahan, 2015, p. 30
12 Van Boven et al., 2018, p. 492
13 Freire, 1970
14 McClure, 2017
15 Gonch, 2016
16 Lindsay, 2020
17 National Council for the Social Studies, 2013
18 Vasilogambros, 2021
19 Pew Research Center, 2021
20 I Side With
21 National Council for the Social Studies, 2013
22 Shapiro & Brown, 2018
23 PBS Newshour, 2020
24 Iyengar et al., 2019
25 Ripley et al., 2019
26 Mutz, 2006, p. 3
27 Finkel et al., 2020, p. 533
28 Hess & McAvoy, 2015, p. 147
29 Druckman et al., 2022, p. 1115
30 National Council for the Social Studies, 2013
31 Shapiro & Brown, 2018
32 Carnegie Corporation of New York CIRCLE, 2003
33 Shapiro & Brown, 2018
34 Abramowitz & Saunders, 2008
35 Mutz, 2006, p. 31
36 Yudkin et al., 2019
37 Ripley et al., 2019
38 I think, but cannot be sure, that she was referring to the Stanford
    initiative called "America in One Room"
        See https://cdd.stanford.edu/2019/america-in-one-room/

4

Cross-Cutting Dialogue Through Cross-Country Connections

In the fall of 2021, I delivered a faculty workshop that left at least one attendee disgruntled. "I am frustrated," the teacher told me, "by all this talk of labels—Republican and Democrat. Our school's mission is to find common ground. Why do you keep talking about division?" My discussion of political polarization had vexed that particular teacher, and his question exposed my oversight. I never explicitly stated what I should have: that we are deeply divided but that, even in the face of division, there is room for hope. We do still share some common bonds, and our divisions are not intractable.

It has been my experience, generally, that schools celebrate diversity, to the chagrin of some parents who seek to minimize the emphasis on difference. The truth is that each of these mindsets—the "salad bowl" worldview of the educators I knew and the "melting pot" mentality of those parents who were sometimes unsettled by aspects of the curriculum—can inform our preparation of students to face a polarized society. It is nearly incontrovertible that elements of difference—such as race—impact how people experience our society; acknowledging difference matters. It is also true, though, that we educators sometimes dwell on difference at the expense of cohesion. We are polarized. But we are not as divided as some might assume, and research shows a benefit to finding our commonalities.

DOI: 10.4324/9781003289494-4

More in Common, as the organization's name optimistically suggests, seeks threads that bind Americans across party affiliation. "One of the many corrosive effects of polarization," they write, "is that it often locks us into thinking in false binaries—leaving us seemingly trapped between two starkly opposed alternatives."[1] Their research finds at least some slivers of unity that transcend politics. An overwhelming majority of Americans express pride in their American identity and gratitude for being able to live in this country, and separate research shows that we tend to exaggerate the depth of the political divide.[2] Common sense suggests that it is worth figuring out what holds us together, even as we bemoan the divisions that drive us apart.

It was in this optimistic spirit that I boarded a plane several years ago and headed south. I was off to build some bridges.

A Cross-Country Partnership

Fresh from the airport, I wandered Birmingham, Alabama as the sun set over what felt like an eerily deserted city, and my imagination filled the space with scenes from *Eyes on the Prize*—Klansmen parading down the sidewalk in defiance of sit-ins and police dogs snarling at protesters. As darkness encroached, I almost expected Bull Connor himself to dart out of the shadows, seize his bullhorn, and order me back onto the plane that had just brought me from Boston. Steeped as I was in the history of the Civil Rights Movement, it felt to me as if I had crossed not only the Mason-Dixon line, but also time itself, turning back the clock on racial progress; because that's what I thought I knew of Birmingham (also known, at one point, as "Bombingham"), Alabama.

I was there to meet a colleague who had agreed to connect his students from the deep South to mine—the "others" in left-leaning, bleeding-heart Massachusetts. We were ready to widen some worldviews, and we were blissfully unburdened by what was at that time unpublished research that might have given us pause. It turns out that mere exposure to "otherness" does not by itself necessarily lead to the sort of empathy and understanding we were after. One 2018 study, for example, found that exposing conservatives to liberal Twitter feeds led the study's participants to grow *more* conservative in their political outlook, rather than more moderate.[3] Despite my rosy outlook for a bold new collaboration, then, I could have made a mess of things by digging my students even deeper into their geographically based trenches. Fortunately, I stumbled my way into a successful partnership.

We began by inviting students to challenge each other's stereotypes. Back in Massachusetts, before breathing a word about what we'd be up to in the coming weeks, I asked my kids what came to mind when I said the words "the South" or "southerners;" my counterpart in Alabama did the same. The stereotypes were regrettable, but perhaps predictable, with many Massachusetts seventh graders thinking of slaves, slavery, and racists. The word Republican was popular, as was Texas (driving the kids in Alabama crazy; one incredulous student asked, "You think TEXAS is in the SOUTH?"). The imagery generated in Alabama was in some cases positive. Still, "rude, weird, annoying, and prissy" were also popular descriptors of northerners. When all students had shared their impressions, each teacher compiled those responses into word clouds, which we then shared with our classes.

FIGURE 4.1

Impressions of the South among northern students

Fortunately, I had the presence of mind to record one of those scenes, which was lively, even by the cacophonous standards of a middle school classroom. My students were mortified by their collective descriptions of southerners. "Oh no! We called them 'racist.' That's so mean!"

"KKK! We said they were in the KKK!"

"Who wrote 'cave?'"

"Mr. Lenci, you're not going to show them this, are you?"

"Yep. Already did!"

Our impressions of the South having been etched into word-cloud infamy, we faced the mirror, turning our attention to southerners' impressions of the North. Indignation prevailed, although it was tempered among some students by a nervous gleefulness. In the video I recorded, the first 30 seconds or so are virtually unintelligible: "WHAT?that'snotevenRUDE!whyw ould?HAAAthat'sfunny!theycalledusWAITthat'sreallyuncalle dforSORUDE!" As the dust settled, distinct reactions emerged. "Misguided? What's that supposed to mean?"

"Diverse. Thank you very much!"

"They said 'liars.' Um. Excuse me?"

"Celtics. Yes! I love the Celtics!"

"Meditative? I'm really confused."

"Selfish? Why did they call us 'selfish'?'"

The scene in Alabama unfolded in similar fashion, with students first viewing the word cloud depicting their own impressions of the North. Embarrassed laughter breaks out at the opening of that session's recording before the first audible reaction rises above the din: "This is so mean! Oh my God!"

"What do you see that's mean?" asks their teacher.

"Prissy. Rich. Rude!" says another student. As had been the case in my classroom, Alabama students were mortified by their associations, and it was with trepidation that they anticipated what was to come. Later in the video, as the teacher is about to reveal to his students the word cloud we northerners created, one boy in the front row unconsciously moves his hand in front of his eyes; he can't bear to look. As with my own students, the outburst is immediate, dominated by laughter. Eventually, one student says, "This is so offensive!"

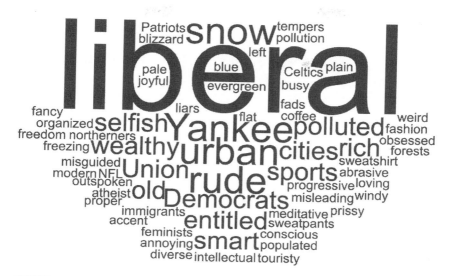

FIGURE 4.2
Southern students' impressions of the North

"What's offensive?" asks the teacher.

"Everything!" respond several students in unison.

Each year of the project, I was struck by the degree to which my students took this exercise personally. They had been asked to respond to an abstract prompt about the "others" across the Mason-Dixon line, as had their counterparts. They did not know these children. In fact, when they completed the initial response, they did not even know they would be collaborating with anyone, anywhere. They simply walked into class the first day after winter vacation and, without warning, were told to take out a piece of paper.

And yet, despite the generalized nature of the prompt— "What comes to mind when I say the words "the South" or "southerners?"—most students interpreted the resulting adjectives as direct, personal descriptors of themselves or the kids with whom they ended up communicating. They wondered why a child in Alabama would call them "weird." When they saw the word "racist" on the word cloud we generated, they winced at having, in their minds, called a particular person in Alabama "racist." It was difficult to disentangle the generalized stereotypes represented in those word clouds from the individuals in each classroom.

This speaks to a finding in the research. Increasingly, political scientists are showing that affective polarization is exacerbated by bad information. According to Doug Ahler and Guarav Sood, Americans have conjured up a stereotypical vision of the political other that does not match reality. Americans believe that nearly half of Republicans earn over $250,000 per year, when in fact only 2% do. People vastly overestimate the number of agnostics and atheists in the Democratic party and also overestimate the percentage of evangelicals among Republicans;[4] Democrats are not as godless as the public generally imagines, nor are Republicans as faithful.

More in Common, too, has documented this phenomenon. In 2019, they asked over 2,000 people a series of questions about immigrants, race, gun control, and other contentious topics. They also asked participants what they believed *others*—those across the political spectrum—thought about the same issues. Their findings: "Americans have a deeply distorted understanding of each other."[5] Democrats underestimated the percentage of Republicans who agreed that racism remains a problem by 28 points. By the same margin, Republicans underestimated the number of Democrats who report being proud Americans. On question after question, the researchers found a gulf between the expectations of one side and the realities reported by the other side. "In essence," writes a separate research team, "people dislike the other party in part because they (inaccurately) perceive it to be quite different from themselves and full of disliked groups."[6] This certainly seemed to be true of my students, who pictured southerners to be racist hillbillies, while their counterparts in Alabama conjured up the elitist, impersonal northerner.

The remedy, according to researchers, is to debunk the stereotypes by revealing the true makeup of the opposing tribe. "Across multiple experiments," say Ahler and Sood, "partisans who receive accurate information about their out-party's composition rate their opposing party's supporters as less extreme and report feeling warmer toward them, suggesting not only a cause of partisanship but also a potential cure for its pathologies."[7] In our case, the "out-party" was geographically defined, and the purpose of our cross-country collaboration was to chip away at the stereotypes that informed students' perceptions of their counterparts across the Mason-Dixon line.

To do so, I started with the low-hanging fruit, showing pictures from my Birmingham trip. The view of the city, which I photographed from the upper levels of a downtown skyscraper, looked nothing like the tumbleweed-strewn desert many of my students had associated with the South. Photos of famous southerners also made a mark: Rosa Parks? Martin Luther King, Jr.? George Washington? These were not the folks my students pictured when they first imagined the "other" across the Mason-Dixon line.

Far more engaging, though, were the video chats we arranged between the two schools, meetings that invariably began with the least threatening topics ("How cold is it there?" "Does it ever snow?"). Sports greased the wheels of discussion, with the University of Alabama having won a national championship the night before one of our discussions and the New England Patriots in the hunt for a Superbowl win. With the ice broken, the conversations turned more profound, and many of my Massachusetts students were surprised to discover that wisdom and southern accents can go hand in hand.

Confederate monuments were in the news one year, with southern municipalities in a bind over the contentious emblems, particularly after the violent attack that took place in Charlottesville, Virginia during the summer of 2017. Some local officials, barred by state law from removing statues, constructed barriers to conceal those statues from public view. Several Alabama students thought that made sense. Another found the barriers misguided, since history should not be erased. Yet another pointed out that the monuments were a celebration of slavery, rather than a neutral guide to history, and therefore did not deserve protection under the guise of historical preservation. My students were surprised by the viewpoint diversity on this topic, having expected a uniform southern perspective.

In addition to the video chats, we established a blog, through which students could communicate asynchronously. Students flooded the pages of that blog with reactions to the word clouds. "Why do you view us as 'proper?' " one asked. "Why do you use the word 'selfish' to describe the North? Is it just a stereotype, or is there some personal reason why you say that?" asked another. Many wanted to know about the word *rude*. "Do you really think of us that way? What have we done to make you say that?" The answer, according to Alabama students, was that they pictured big northern cities as crowded cells of jostling humanity— exemplified by the traffic of mid-town Manhattan, featured in so many movies that it had come to represent the North more generally. In turn, my students conceded that they had prob- ably leaned on unflattering media that depicted southerners as toothless hillbillies.[8]

Beyond the initial interrogation of stereotypes, the pro- ject succeeded because it involved a shared task. Decades ago, Gordon Allport proposed that hostility between competing groups could be softened through intergroup contact if that con- tact met a handful of conditions,[9] one of which was a common goal. Like most of my moves as a teacher, I knew nothing about this research when I designed the project, but it seemed to make sense to have kids from Alabama and Massachusetts work together on the same project. So, that's what we did.

Having moved past the personal introductions, students turned to the constitutionality of banning the Confederate battle flag in schools. Each student in Alabama and Massachusetts served in one of three capacities in prepar- ation for our mock Supreme Court hearings: as attorneys representing a Tennessee student punished for brandishing a Confederate flag in school, as attorneys for that school, or as Supreme Court Justices deciding the case.[10] Bowing to logistical challenges, students mainly worked with their own classmates on this task, but through the blog they also consulted their counterparts across the Mason-Dixon line, swapping research leads and testing legal theories. Each school essentially ran the project in parallel to soften the scheduling headaches while allowing for a degree of cooperation and consultation as students made their way, roughly in concert, though the project from across the country.

Along the way, students cemented their impressions of their counterparts across the Mason-Dixon line as knowledgeable resources, rather than backward, southern hicks or impersonal, northern automatons. When learners in one school hit a dead end, others seemed to have a lead, and the diverse educational and experiential backgrounds on either side of the Mason-Dixon line made the endeavor richer than it could have been had either school tackled the project alone. One year, a southern student talked about the reverence with which his family treated a battle flag that had been passed down through the generations. Another year, Massachusetts students shared their offense at having seen a Confederate flag flying on Martin Luther King Day. The conversation was richer for its variety.

Students Discover a Connection

As is often the case with teaching, one of the most revealing moments of the project emerged despite—not because of—me and my rules. I was grouchy one day, frustrated by glitchy technology and irritated when, minutes into a video chat, I caught two students messing around. They were holding their hands next them, forefingers touching thumbs in what looked like an upside-down "OK" sign. Halfway across the country, kids giggled in response. "What are you doing?" I hissed.

"We're trying to get them to look."

"What do you mean, you're 'trying to get them to look?' Stop 'trying to get them to look.' We're already looking at each other. What does that even mean?"

"It's a game. You just hold up your hand like this and try to get the other person to look." I was suspicious. Was it a lewd reference? "No, Mr. Lenci, you just try to get people to look."

"Why?"

"Because that's the point of the game."

"But how do they know this game?"

"Everyone knows!" By "everyone," they meant kids, and in short order, students in Alabama and Massachusetts had reframed the narrative. No longer were they "northerners" and "southerners," separated by distance and historical legacy. Instead, they were digital natives whose common currency—probably

YouTube—had at some point introduced them to this inane activity—a game to which I, the unsavvy elder, was not privy. I was witnessing the effect of what psychologists call "common ingroup identity," in which in-group and out-group references fade in the presence of some unifying sense of community. For a few minutes, freed from my carefully planned intellectual pursuits, "northern" and "southern" labels receded, replaced by the bond of being a kid.

It is still possible for Americans to find these commonalities. Matthew Levendusky has discovered that on and around the Fourth of July, people feel less animosity toward the opposing political camp than is the case throughout the rest of the year. The holiday, says Levendusky, serves as a prompt to remind Americans of their shared identity. To engender cooperation, rather than competition, Levendusky recommends reminding people of these shared bonds. "Normally, when a Democrat thinks about Republicans, her partisan identity is her most salient identity, stemming from its centrality to political thinking in the American context. As a result, she sees Republicans as members of a disliked out-group and evaluates them negatively."[11] The cure, says Levendusky, is to shift the mental frame. It is impossible to erase the human inclination to create us/them dichotomies. The trick is to leverage that instinct by switching up what we consider to be our team.

In retrospect, I suppose I had primed my students to associate southerners with slavery. This was, after all, a history class, and slavery had been a point of discussion during the constitutional studies that had preceded our collaboration. I thought I'd been clever by springing the word-cloud activity on them immediately after vacation, when two weeks of unmoderated screen time had burnished their minds to a dull, blank sheen. But this was still history class, and they were poised to ingest information through that lens, which they pointed out in their written reflections. "As a lot of people in our class have said," wrote one student toward the end of the project, "we made this word cloud with the Civil War in mind, which definitely made me think of slavery." Still, my students managed to overcome my unintentional framing of the experience as a battlefield standoff, simply by making an upside-down "OK" sign: they were kids first, northerners second.

Shanto Iyengar, like Levendusky, emphasizes the value in finding commonalities, rather than exclusively focusing on differences. "When we bring forward what unites Democrats and Republicans, rather than emphasizing what divides and separates them, partisan animus subsides."[12] I bear witness to the fact that the effect holds true for students when the fault line is not politics, per se, but instead geographical divide. Whether through the discovery of shared musical tastes, or sports references, or a diversion that remained all but inscrutable to their teacher, the project served as a bridge across distance and culture.

On balance, the collaboration worked. After several weeks of engagement with their counterparts in the South, my students saw things in a new light. They had been mortified by the word cloud they created in the early days of the collaboration, and I now realize their chagrin was mostly about conflict avoidance. My students did, in fact, initially think of the South as the home of racism and racists—they just did not want to admit it to any southerners. Each year, though, students came to realize they had overgeneralized. "Most of us at Brookwood probably haven't even met a person from the South," one student wrote in a reflection, "so almost all of our words were stereotypes." Even assuming that I was told some of what I wanted to hear, the feedback was overwhelmingly positive: kids loved talking to their counterparts in Alabama, whom they found engaging, thoughtful, and fun.

Because the Confederate flag took center stage in our collaboration, students' thinking gravitated toward the legacy of slavery and the Civil War. "When we first started this project," wrote one seventh grader, "I thought that most people in the South still had the idea of slavery and weren't that accepting of other races. I now see that I was completely wrong." In one of my class sections, almost every student recalled the same moment from a video call to illustrate how their thinking about southerners had changed. A student in Massachusetts had asked what people in Alabama thought of the Confederate flag. "I am disgusted by it," answered a Birmingham student. This response captivated my kids, who had expected to find either support for, or at least equivocation about, the Confederate flag among southerners. "I was surprised one student thought that the confederate flag was 'disgusting,' and the majority of them didn't like it," wrote one of my students. "They said they wished it wasn't part of their past…. I thought that the confederate flag would be more of a symbol of the south, and their home, and less of something they hated."[13]

For many of my students, the most profound insight was that there is no single "southerner." Some southerners might still cherish—or at least tolerate—the Confederate flag, but some clearly despised it. Many students in this Alabama classroom cheered for the Alabama Crimson Tide. But one was more interested in basketball, rooting for, of all teams, the Boston Celtics. "When we first started this project," wrote a northern student, "I thought *no one is going to be against the Confederate flag in the South because they are united there*, but now I understand that the South is just as divided in these big issues as the North is." The recognition that the South is not a monolithic culture—the discovery of nuance—allowed my students to break out of the confines of a uniformly "us" versus "them" dichotomy.

Curricular Resources for Cross-Country Collaborations

The only real drawback of that two-week project was the labor of sustaining a cross-country collaboration—particularly building and maintaining the shared blog. Fortunately, new resources promise to ease that load. During my final months as a teacher, I was introduced to the folks at AllSides for Schools ("preparing students for thoughtful participation in democracy—and in life"[14]), who had been building the technological infrastructure that would pair classrooms across the country to encourage dialogue across lines of difference. They called this project Mismatch, and my class was among the first to pilot the program in the spring of 2018. We were connected to a school in North Carolina, and students joined together with two or three partners to discuss the limits of the First Amendment. Our experience was fleeting, but it hinted at the promise of things to come: organizations connecting students across distance or ideological divide to facilitate dialogue and mutual understanding.

Courtesy of the pandemic, the ubiquity of video-conference platforms may bring similar conversations more easily within reach, and several organizations facilitate intranational conversations that should appeal to teachers looking to expose their students to different points of view. American Pals revives the tried-and-true pen pal model to "bridge divides and connect America's classrooms, one letter at a time,"[15] while the American Exchange Project organizes cross-country travel. "By bringing together high school students from across the country," they write, "we are exposing the next generation of voters to perspectives and ideas they won't get anywhere else."[16] The National Constitution Center connects middle and upper school students with peers across the country to discuss constitutional issues.[17]

During the summer of 2021, I presented a workshop to earnest college students doing their best to ease the crisis of political polarization. The Panorama Project was the brainchild of a talented team of students and recent graduates of Carlton College, and they had recruited several dozen participants from across the country to explore the causes of and solutions to polarization. Along the way, they invited a handful of outside speakers to share their knowledge, and participants worked in small groups throughout the summer to distill their learning. The endeavor was well organized and populated by thoughtful participants. It is yet another example of a national coalition of learners—in this case at the university level—that could provide inspiration for K-12 teachers looking to broaden the worldviews of their students.

Conclusion: Connect Classrooms to Begin Depolarization

Political polarization is a national plague. The health of our democracy compels us to empower today's students to be the more tolerant, cooperative, and empathetic citizens of tomorrow. Experience has taught me, though, that many educators are paralyzed by politics, and for many, the prospect of intentionally introducing it into the curriculum is simply untenable. However, preparing children for the cross-cutting political talk in which they will engage as adults does not necessarily require us to stick them in "political" discussions today. They don't need to argue as seventh graders about who should be president in order to practice the skills that will eventually position them to navigate our polarized society. They do need practice, though, at communicating and cooperating with people who may at first glance appear to be dissimilar or disagreeable to them.

The collaboration that my students experienced was not based in political difference, per se, yet it will help prepare them to deal with political difference. This is how learning works. We introduce four-year-olds to numbers, and years later they learn electrical engineering. We teach them letters and they later write novels. We connect them with a classroom full of kids from a different part of the country who have absorbed different values or different cultural reference points, and, having been exposed to those people, they add a bit more to the civic foundation that will allow them to mend our political divide one day.

And, as the following chapter contends, we have them turn to each other, within their own classrooms, for the same purpose.

Notes

1   Hawkins & Raghuram, 2020, p. 5
2   Ahler & Sood, 2018
3   Bail et al., 2018
4   Ahler & Sood, 2018
5   More in Common, 2019
6   Iyengar et al., 2019, p. 140
7   Ahler & Sood, 2018, p. 2
8   During the first couple of years of the project, two television shows—*Duck Dynasty* and *Here Comes Honey Boo Boo*—were in the public consciousness. Each offered a healthy serving of southern stereotypes, and many of my students cited one or the other as a source of their "information" about southerners. Countless video

clips scattered across the internet and social media seemed to also inform my students' impressions of southerners as backward rednecks

9 Nickerson, 2021

10 As of now, the blogs that anchored the project are still accessible online. Readers who are interested in learning more about the details of the mock hearing will find several video clips memorializing students' arguments and their reflections on the verdicts. The blogs from the three school years, beginning with 2016–2017, can be found in the appendix

11 Levendusky, 2018, p. 61

12 Iyengar et al., 2019, p. 140

13 For more reactions, see the blog: https://brookwoodschool.net/blogs/masondixon1819/2019/01/18/chatting-with-highlands/#comments

14 AllSides for Schools, 2021

15 American Pals

16 American Exchange Project, 2020

17 National Constitution Center, 2022

5

Teaching Students to Build Bridges Within the Classroom

As exciting as it was to collaborate with students in Alabama, viewpoint diversity exists closer to home, as well. Several years ago, four of my seventh-grade students declared themselves citizens of a newly formed Republic of Utah and arranged their desks to claim this autonomous enclave within the borders of my classroom. We had studied the Electoral College, and the reliably conservative voting history of the state called to these kids. Utah seemed like their kind of place. They staked their claim to this island of conservatism amid a sea of progressive politics and let us know that, if we needed them, we could find them in Utah.

Surveys performed by Paula McAvoy and Diana Hess, authors of the book *The Political Classroom*, reveal that most classrooms feature viewpoint diversity[1]—even those classrooms (like mine in left-leaning Massachusetts) that appear ideologically homogenous. McAvoy and Hess claim that students are well served when they "discuss and deliberate controversial political issues,"[2] but how, exactly, do we make that happen? How do we help kids build bridges between islands of ideology— between the Utahs of our classrooms and the rest of the room? It begins by establishing norms of behavior that convince students their voices are welcome, even when their ideas are unpopular. It includes instruction on good listening habits, and it calls for

DOI: 10.4324/9781003289494-5

teachers to reconsider what makes a "class discussion." Finally, it requires us to assess student mastery of what we say we value.

Establishing Classroom Norms

When I deliver workshops, I often hear the same question: *how do I get them all to talk*? The ideological minority of a classroom tends to stay quiet, leading to a frustrating bind: educators agree in principle that exposure to cross-cutting dialogue provides important training for students, but their conversations, plagued by accord, stall; the kids who might have a different angle to offer often keep it to themselves.

Students rarely share their thoughts with a hostile crowd. Consequently, productive dialogue begins with a positive school culture in which students truly believe their ideas and opinions are honored, even when those viewpoints run contrary to those of the majority. The transformative dialogue of a mid-winter unit is enabled by the preceding, months-long effort to develop a welcoming classroom culture. There are tools to help us get there.

Facing History and Ourselves offers one of those resources— a well-conceived protocol for establishing a classroom contract governing how people treat each other in the classroom. The framework avoids edicts, instead inviting students and teachers to co-create the contract; the agreement has teeth because all parties have a stake in it. The contracting experience begins by asking students to reflect on times when they have felt comfortable speaking up in class, invites students to conceive of important behavioral norms, and shares several norms that have been used in previous Facing History classrooms. Alternatively, the protocol invites students to reflect on hypothetical scenarios to generate behavioral norms ("*When we have an idea but do not feel comfortable sharing it out loud, we can...*"[3]). The product of this work is the foundation upon which the business of human interaction rests for the remainder of the year; it's the rules of the road.

Learning for Justice, too, has an excellent guide called *Let's Talk*[4] that includes a section entitled "Laying the Groundwork for Critical Conversations." It offers a simple framework, easily implemented among younger or older students, for establishing classroom norms based on how students want the class to sound, look, and feel, and it encourages students to face the uneasiness of challenging dialogue. "Remember," says the guide, "that feeling safe and valued are not the same as feeling comfortable."[5] As with Facing History's framework, the strength of the agreement rests on a foundation of collaboration.

Some schools establish norms of community engagement that transcend individual classrooms. Brookwood School, where I worked, articulated a simple set of expectations that applied to all members of the community,[6] two of which— *I communicate respectfully, directly, and clearly* and *I honor differences and diverse perspectives*—are particularly relevant to depolarization. The Mission in Practice was posted at the front of my and every other classroom, reminding community members of our shared expectations of and commitment to each other. Before ever finding themselves in a "political" conversation with me, students had honored others' points of view in previous years and believed, therefore, that theirs would also be honored.

Whether within a classroom or, more ambitiously, at the schoolwide level, educators must establish the foundational practices and protocols upon which the cross-cutting political dialogue that McAvoy and Hess propose could rest. Or, to put it a bit more forcefully, there's little reason to expect productive dialogue across lines of disagreement in the absence of that groundwork.

Teaching Students How to Listen

Establishing classroom—or schoolwide—norms is a prerequisite for entering into dialogue across lines of difference, but without specific instruction, those norms will remain merely aspirational. Children need to know the nuts and bolts of how to talk to each other productively.

A year or two ago, I was preparing to deliver a workshop on contentious conversations in the classroom. I had proposed including the topic of listening, which caused my host to wrinkle her nose. "I think folks have heard about listening before," she told me. "What else do you have?" Indeed, it is old news, yet listening remains the "special sauce" in reaching across lines of disagreement, according to Amanda Ripley, author of *High Conflict*.[7] One of the country's most prominent bridge-building alliances is known as the Listen First Project.[8] Across the many books and innumerable studies I read while researching this project, one simple, intuitive reminder kept reasserting itself: if we are serious about reaching across lines of divide, we need to listen—really listen—to the other side.

Wisdom abounds when it comes to listening. Tania Israel, author of the book *Beyond Your Bubble: How to Connect Across the Political Divide*, distills it to three active skills: nonverbal attending, reflecting, and asking open-ended questions.[9] Douglas Stone and Sheila Heen, in their book *Thanks for the Feedback*, say that listening includes asking questions, paraphrasing, and recognizing emotions.[10] In a widely viewed Ted Talk, Celeste Headlee claims that there's no need to act as if you're listening... "if you're actually listening!"[11] Despite some differences in approach among these and other experts, common themes emerge: great listening includes discrete elements that reinforce each other and that require practice and concentration to deploy effectively. This stuff takes work.

Bill Ivey, a teacher and middle school dean at Stoneleigh-Burnham School in Massachusetts, teaches listening through a framework he adapted from the book *Basic Attending Skills*, by Allen E. Ivey, Norma Gluckstein Packard, and Mary Bradford Ivey. Bill and his colleague, Amanda Mozea, introduce their middle school students to the mechanics of listening within a seminar called "Discovery" that consolidates what Bill refers to as "life skills." The first listening skill, attending, includes elements such as eye contact and body language. The second is learning to extend an "open invitation to talk" through the use of open-ended questions. The use of encouragers (such as a noncommittal "hmmm") constitutes the third skill, with paraphrasing, reflecting feelings, and summarizing rounding out the remainder of the framework.

Like Israel and Ivey, Simon Greer, founder of Bridging the Gap, conceives of listening as the culmination of several distinct elements, each of which I practiced in a 2022 workshop delivered by Greer.[12] It felt awkward to remain utterly silent for several minutes as I listened to a partner describe his ideal meal and unnatural, too, to initially remain in the "footprint," as Greer calls it, of my partner's words by strictly reflecting back what he had said. In my discomfort, though, I was reminded that listening is work and that, after 20 years as a teacher, I still had work to do.

The capacity to maintain silence and the inclination to stay with the speaker, rather than push the conversation elsewhere, pave the way for the remaining elements of Greer's framework, which call for a more active approach on the part of the listener. "Encouragers" include nonverbal cues (nodding, raising an eyebrow) and succinct verbal responses ("wow!"). Asking open-ended questions such as "What was that like for you?" marks the fourth element of the framework, with "sorting, grouping, and synthesizing"—helping the listener find patterns in what they have said—the fifth.

The most valuable lesson I gleaned from Greer is that listeners tend to shape the course of conversations more than they suspect. We send signals when we listen—wincing slightly at an unwelcome comment or nodding at something that resonates. A truly great listener, says Greer, will learn to encourage the speaker to go where *they* want the conversation to head by expending every ounce of energy required to discern—through painstaking, committed listening—which direction that might be.

Despite Headlee's observation that good listening advertises itself, researchers have uncovered specific language that helps us indicate that our minds are open for business. Harvard researcher Julia Minson is among the academics to have identified a trait called "receptiveness," which is defined as opening oneself to ideas or information that challenge existing beliefs[13]—essentially the opposite of the identity-protective reasoning that can sabotage a reasoned exchange.

Interestingly, even people who are cognitively receptive, says Minson, may appear disinterested to their conversational partner. Using certain words and phrases can correct this misperception, raising the level of discourse and actually causing the conversational partner to grow more receptive in return. "It's contagious,"[14] says Minson. "The most important signal of receptiveness involves acknowledging your counterpart's point of view: 'I understand you're saying ...' or 'I think you mentioned ...' In other words, actively showing that you heard what the other person said."[15] Minson's finding is in concert with a theme that runs through the literature on this topic: listening is ultimately an active sport.

For many teachers, a review of listening skills is nothing revelatory. The advice of the experts and researchers merely confirms what most of us instinctively sense through our daily human interactions in schools—that a free exchange of ideas requires open dialogue and that the listening that fuels dialogue takes active work. Still, many of us forget to overtly teach and reinforce these skills with students. If we are serious about preparing them to ease the country's polarization, we must.

Curricular Resources to Encourage Dialogue

The specific language cited by Julia Minson as a tool of conversational receptiveness is remarkably similar to wording in the latter half of the *Let's Talk* guide from Learning for Justice, which provides concrete linguistic guidance for students. A list of sentence stems in that resource—including "What did you mean when you mentioned...?" and "I agree and would add..."[16]—tees up the specific language to grease the wheels of dialogue.

The *Bridging Differences Playbook*, a product of the Greater Good Science Center, includes similar modeling. The playbook is divided into three sections—intrapersonal skills, interpersonal skills, and intergroup skills to foster bridge-building. The first exercise in the interpersonal section is called *Listen with Compassion*. "We're more likely to want to bridge our differences with someone when we feel heard and understood by them," reads the resource, "—and we're more effective at communicating with someone when we really listen to where they're coming from." The playbook offers a number of wording suggestions, including open-ended questions such as "When you say_____, do you mean_____?" It also reminds students to try phrases such as "that makes sense" or "I hear you."[17] As with the resource from Learning for Justice, the guide arms educators with simple but effective language to help students reach across lines of divide.

The curricular resources from Learning for Justice and The Greater Good Science Center help us support students in their bridge-building efforts, as would a guide I created in partnership with the Better Arguments Project (BAP). One of many organizations working to bridge the political gap, the Better Arguments Project seeks "to help bridge divides—not by papering over these divides but by helping people have better arguments."[18] Five principles anchor their approach: *take winning off the table; prioritize relationships and listen passionately; pay attention to context; embrace vulnerability;* and *make room to transform.* I was introduced to the Better Arguments Project in my final months as a classroom teacher, and as the walls of the pandemic closed in, I took to my laptop and helped that organization apply their principles to the classroom.

The result of that collaboration is a curriculum for middle and high school students.[19] Broken into six sessions, the resource uses the five principles to provoke increasingly sophisticated approaches to engaging in dialogue. One session, for example, encourages students to embrace the organization's first tenet— "take winning off the table." Henri Tajfel would approve. "Lead with a desire to understand and learn," suggests the BAP, "rather than win." To help students do so, the curriculum presents an ambiguous illustration and asks them to appreciate how it might be viewed by someone else. Understanding, not winning, becomes the goal. Subsequent lessons in the Better Arguments curriculum, such as "prioritize relationships and listen passionately," provide further levels of structure to enhance conversations across lines of disagreement.

In similar fashion, OpenMind, an organization that "explores the inner working of the mind and the psychological roots of our differences," provides an online curriculum to help students navigate ideological divides.[20] The curriculum opens with explanatory lessons on the causes of our divisions before introducing tools to bridge the divide. In total, eight sessions comprise this curriculum that, while intended for older students—those in high school in college—could also be modified by those who teach younger students.

Practicing Dialogue in the Classroom

We educators must help our students establish norms of behavior that will invite cross-cutting dialogue, and we must also teach them specific communication skills to employ in their exchanges. But how do we orchestrate those exchanges? The middle school students I taught always hankered for a good fight. Apropos of nothing, they would sometimes bounce into my room at the start of class and, armed with the unshakable faith that today might just be the day, ask if they could have a debate. "Come oooooon, Mr. Lenci! Can we?"

And why wouldn't they? A debate delivers what they crave—a team, joined together in solidarity, with a clear enemy to contest (again, recall Tajfel). I was a perpetual disappointment though, in that proper debates were vanishingly rare in my classroom. As Chapter Three indicates, research shows that we tend to discredit or discard credible information that challenges our deeply held beliefs, meaning that human nature leaves little room to be convinced by a debate point. Training students to defend their arguments has unquestionable merit as a basis for a host of intellectual endeavors, but we should not assume that such training prepares students to bridge the ideological or political divide. If not debate, though, what does it look like to engage across that chasm?

In my 20 years in the classroom, I facilitated a number of lively class discussions. Those conversations, on gun control or the racial divide or the early polling numbers from battleground states, crackled with energy and assured me that, whatever else might be going wrong that day, those kids were really learning. Eventually, though, I came to appreciate the classroom dynamics that, in turn, tempered my celebratory outlook.

In a full-group class discussion, it is almost always the case that a handful of extroverted and articulate students will dominate the discussion, to the exclusion of the majority of the class. What might feel to a teacher like a "great discussion" among a room full of students may, upon reflection, be more realistically characterized as a supercharged exchange among three or four kids, with a handful of others, like closely orbiting planets, feeling the warmth of that energy. The rest of the classroom universe, though, looks on from afar.

There are ways to encourage broader participation among a large group. The Harkness methodology, for example, encourages older students, traditionally arranged around a circular table, to engage each other directly, often with little interference from a teacher. It can be tricky for many teachers, though, to arrange their furniture and bodies in a way that engenders meaningful exchanges among the entirety of the class community. For me, it is ultimately a matter of math: students get more practice communicating when they are partnered with a small number of their peers. As a teacher, I do not always need to hear what they're saying for the discussion to have value.

Small Groupings for More Dialogic Practice

There are many ways to break down the numbers. Think-pair-shares provide a structured exchange among dyads who consider a conversation prompt before exchanging ideas with a partner and then opening themselves up for a larger discussion. In a tower of talk,[21] students begin with colored cubes and add their color to a shared tower that visually logs the balanced contributions of the team. In another approach, students can be assigned roles—timekeeper, scribe, facilitator—within a small group. I tended to seat my students in groups of four, finding that such an arrangement provided each group enough voices for conversational energy, yet few enough to encourage uniform participation.

Telling someone else's story can be a powerful form of cross-cutting dialogue. The film *Dialogue Lab: America* highlights the use of this technique among adults who came together across the political spectrum to engage in civil dialogue during the summer of 2021,[22] and the same process works in the classroom.

Sven Holch, a former colleague and fellow middle school teacher, assigns students a preparatory reading on one side of a contentious issue and then partners them with a counterpart who received literature on the opposing side. In conversation, a student explains the side they were assigned, listens carefully as their partner does the same, and synthesizes the information to formulate their own viewpoint on the matter. When each member of the dyad has shared their opinion, the partner reports to the whole class the *other* person's perspective.

There are limitations to the use of partnerships or small-group discussions in the classroom. When the moment calls for a broader gathering, though, there are still ways to structure the conversation so that it is not dominated by a vocal minority. Fishbowls place a small cohort at the center of a room as other students surround that core group and carefully observe the conversation. Another strategy is to arrange students in concentric circles, facing each other, so that after one exchange, all students within one circle slide over a chair to meet a new conversational partner.[23] Physical movement can also be leveraged in a "four corners" exercise that asks students to move to a part of the room that indicates their level of agreement to a given statement. In an "anonymized debate," all members of a class jot down their thoughts in response to a discussion prompt. The index cards are then shuffled, and each student selects a card and shares the perspective depicted on that card.[24]

Classroom dialogue need not even include the spoken word. Good, old-fashioned writing still works, such as asking students to respond to a prompt on Post-it notes that they then stick on the wall for subsequent analysis, sorting, and reflection by classmates. And technology continues to deliver ever-expanding options to engage in dialogue, such as the blog my students maintained with their counterparts in Alabama or the back-channel conversations that run in parallel to a video call. Students who remain on the sidelines of a full-class verbal exchange often find their voices through the written word.

In short, the answer to the question, *How do I get them all to talk?* is to reconsider what it means to talk. A single classroom conversation in which the teacher serves as facilitator can be severely limiting. There is certainly a time for such exchanges, but if we want students to get in their reps—their practice at communicating across lines of difference and disagreement—we must draw from a wider menu of options that includes small-group discussions, structured exchanges within the full class, and written communication.

Assessment of Bridge-Building Skills

Our students must practice the foundational listening and speaking skills that will equip them to reach across lines of divide. Thoughtful resources lie at the ready to help teachers incorporate such skills into their classrooms, and those curricular materials can more broadly provide a backbone to give students practice in reaching across lines of divide. It is left to us, though, to make sure we account for the extent to which students actually develop those skills.

My experience suggests a mismatch between our aspirations for students and our assessment of them. We encourage kids to "respect differences" and "appreciate different points of view," yet when it comes time to render judgement on their interpersonal interactions, we rely on tired metrics of class participation. Teachers generally reward students for the quantity and volume of their contributions to class discussions, leading to that lamentable pattern of a handful of extroverted, confident, or inquisitive students dominating the airtime. Instead, our assessment of students should reflect what we say we prize. If we indeed aspire for students to navigate the political divide, we must measure their mastery of the particular communication skills that will position them to do so. This is what "class participation" should mean—less pontification, more pondering. When we teachers show kids that communicating effectively across lines of divide matters, they will pay attention.

I recently led a workshop for teachers, during which one of the grade-level teaching teams generated a simple class-participation rubric tethered to the five principles of the Better Arguments Project. This took them 15 minutes to complete. Moving forward, students at that school will be measured against the standards of good listening. They will be judged on whether their words indicate that they enter into dialogue in good faith, having "taken winning off the table." The most extroverted or confident among them may not necessarily take top marks, but those who practice the skills required to reach across lines of divide will.

Feedback need not (and should not) be confined to grading. In a 2020 essay for *Independent School Magazine*, history teacher Robert von Glahn described his efforts to help students develop a degree of self-awareness about their class presence through one-on-one discussions. He shared with students not only instances in which he saw them practicing civility and respect in their interactions but also occasions in which they interrupted others, listened to respond rather than to understand, and generally hogged the spotlight. "At times," wrote von Glahn, "these conversations were difficult.... The students had never received feedback like this before (nor had I ever given it), and some were shaken when they realized the habits they had formed."[25] The work paid off, though, according to von Glahn, with classroom exchanges assuming a more civil tone by mid-year.

Digital Portfolios

Teachers must offer explicit feedback to students, but the most impactful feedback will be that which is intrinsic, rather than extrinsic; students must engage in some self-reflection. And because learning to depolarize is an ambitious goal, requiring ample practice across the disciplines and years of schooling, it would make sense for students to have a mechanism that helps them see the breadth of this journey. A sensible solution is a digital portfolio.

This voyage begins with our youngest students, as Karen Shorr, a deeply respected, recently retired teacher of pre-kindergarten (and former colleague), taught me. In Karen's ample experience, disagreement is a predictable feature of lower-elementary classrooms, presenting itself in settings as mundane as a math lesson. When one student, who knows that three plus three equals six, doubts a classmate who claims the answer is reached by adding four plus two, "that's when the learning begins," says Karen. "You have to take the time to have the conversation, to help them see there are various ways to get to six, rather than a single right and wrong way."[26]

Listening provides an indispensable tonic for that disagreement. Karen and her colleagues would model respectful listening for weeks before introducing their students to two special sticks. A star atop one of those sticks encouraged whoever held it to be a "star listener," while the other featured a heart, a reminder to "speak from the heart."[27] A child who wished to communicate something important would seize those sticks and deploy them in conversation. As any teacher of young children knows, listening, like math or science, must be taught and practiced.

Because I was lucky enough to work with elementary school teachers and among their students (who then became my students) for many years, I too understand this, and I know that many teachers of young children deliver the necessary instruction. At some point—possibly when students move from the elementary model of a homeroom teacher to the specialization of middle and high school, the thread can be lost. Learning becomes more subject centered, less student oriented, and the focus on community-building that comes so naturally to elementary school teachers fades into the shadow of discrete academic disciplines—math and science and history.

A portfolio, built over several years of schooling, could be an antidote to this loss of cohesion. The Association of American Colleges and Universities considers the use of digital portfolios a "high-impact practice" (HIP), one of 11 pedagogical tools shown to effectively engage learners.[28] A scholarly journal focuses exclusively on research regarding the use of digital portfolios in education,[29] and a number of companies make it easy for teachers or students to create digital portfolios.[30] People often tout listening as a cornerstone of constructive dialogue, before saying, "It's so important, and yet most of us never learn how to do it." In my experience, that may not be true. What *is* probably true, though, is that the lessons learned at an early age are not explicitly reinforced. One fairly simple way to do so would be to equip our students with a mechanism that helps them recognize the spiraling, reinforcing nature of lessons that are preparing them to meet the demands of a polarized society.

Conclusion: Building Toward Depolarization Within the Classroom

Years from now, our students will assume the weight of seemingly intractable dilemmas facing a fractured society, and their success or failure in managing those challenges will require a capacity to engage with the political or ideological "other." For now, though, they're just kids.

Just as we do not expect children to perform surgery or compose a symphony in second grade, we also do not expect them to solve today's political problems. When we partner students from Alabama with their counterparts in Massachusetts, we do so to give them practice reaching across lines of divide, even if those divisions are not overtly political. When we turn our attention to our own classrooms and the interactions between our own students, we maintain a similar mindset—seeking to provide the building blocks that will support students as they learn to engage across lines of divide, even if their discourse is not what most people would characterize as political.

Those building blocks include establishing norms of behavior that allow children the freedom to explore ideas amongst one another, even when they suspect that their viewpoint is not shared. They include explicit instruction in the communication skills required to reach across lines of divide, as well as opportunities to practice those skills. And to ensure those building blocks are sturdy, we keep an eye on students' development of those skills, let them know how they're faring, and encourage them to monitor their own progress. The development of this self-awareness is an element of social emotional learning, which, in concert with media literacy, provides the focus of Chapter Six.

Notes

1   Hess & McAvoy, 2015
2   McAvoy & Hess, 2013, p. 20
3   Facing History and Ourselves, 2022
4   Learning for Justice
5   Learning for Justice, p. 24
6   Brookwood's complete Mission in Practice reads:

> *I communicate respectfully, directly, and clearly.*
> *I collaborate a t school and in the world.*
> *I think critically, creatively, and globally.*
> *I honor differences and diverse perspectives.*
> *I take risks and when I struggle or fail, I grow more resilient.*
> *I take responsibility for myself, the care of others, and my*
> *environment.*

7   O'Connor & Lawson, 2021
8   Listen First Project, 2021
9   Israel, 2020
10 Stone & Heen, 2014, p. 233
11 Headlee, 2015
12 To read about this approach, see Greer, 2021
13 Minson et al., 2020
14 Minson, 2021
15 Staff, 2021
16 Learning for Justice, p. 24
17 Greater Good Science Center, p. 44
18 The Better Arguments Project, 2020 "Our Approach"
19 The Better Arguments Project, 2020 "Our Resources"
20 OpenMind "Library"
21 McCormick in Middle
22 Pickett & Lawes, 2022
23 Gonzales, 2015
24 Banke, 2020
25 von Glahn, 2020
26 Shorr, 2021

27   Karen often turned to the Center for Healthy Minds (University of Wisconsin-Madison) for activities and inspiration, which is where she found the idea for the "star" and "heart" sticks

28   Kuh, 2008

29   American Association of Colleges and Universities, 2022

30   Seesaw, Digication, and Spikeview are examples

6

Depolarization Requires Managing Media and Emotions

In the spring of 2020, I led a workshop for New England teachers in anticipation of the presidential election. Attendees imagined how they might handle different scenarios come November, including the hypothetical prospect of a student donning a MAGA hat in celebration of a Trump victory. "I would freeze," one teacher said simply. This honest response speaks to the central role of emotions in navigating political or ideological divides. We may plan to our hearts' content—by establishing norms of conversation and implementing listening protocols and modeling language—and we may all—teachers and students alike—muster the most earnest commitment to bridging the divide, and yet we may, despite all of it, freeze in the face of challenge. Or say something impulsive. Or in some other way mess it up. In the words of Mike Tyson, "Everyone has a plan until they get punched in the mouth."[1]

It's not our fault. We're wired that way. Social threats, such as those we perceive from the political "other," trigger physiological responses akin to those elicited by physical threats. Automatic processes inform our thinking. We intend to be measured and rational in our dialogue across lines of difference, but we cannot escape the ancient wiring that causes us to fight, flee, or freeze. We can, however, better position ourselves to productively manage situations that initially feel threatening—and we can

DOI: 10.4324/9781003289494-6

help students do this. Consequently, a holistic approach to preparing students to reach across lines of divide requires attention to social emotional learning (SEL).

It also requires a serious commitment to media literacy, which is inextricably intertwined with social and emotional components. The battle lines of our political disfunction increasingly slice through the media we consume and produce for news and companionship, and students will need to not only understand the role of media in exacerbating polarization but also adopt a critical and curious mindset in managing their media diet. They must learn to use media for their purposes rather than allow themselves to be used by it—as we adults increasingly have allowed ourselves to be.

Emotions Matter

A few years ago, I sat in my classroom, fidgeting. It was June. The students were gone, yet we adults remained. Feeling somewhat sorry for ourselves, with year-end comments still to be written, a group of faculty members had gathered for a workshop delivered by an outside presenter who was speaking of elephants. And riders of elephants. It was a metaphor, one that I struggled to follow. Like the students who had recently sat in that very seat, I was crabby, ready to be elsewhere, although, inconveniently, I was the one who had arranged the workshop. My cognition was a bit addled by my emotional state, which, it turns out, was sort of the point of the presentation: emotion and thinking are inseparable.

It was not until I read Jonathan Haidt's *The Righteous Mind* that I understood what I could not seem to grasp that day in June. Haidt devotes the first third of his book to developing the metaphor of our cognitive processes as an elephant taking a walk. On the elephant's back sits a rider, and the rider likes to think she's in control. Nonetheless, the elephant heads pretty much where he pleases, and the rider, perhaps one day finding herself in a muddy river, says, "Ah yes, here we are! Now we can have a bath!" The elephant in Haidt's metaphor represents the brain's automatic processes—intuition and emotion—while the rider represents controlled processes—reasoning.[2] We like to think the rider, rational and logical, makes the navigational decisions, when in fact she's often reduced to justifying the moves the elephant makes along the way. Emotion is central to thinking.

It is important, then, to understand the intensity of emotion that can be associated with one's political identity. Just as Americans universally recall where we were on September 11, 2001, I distinctly remember watching the news footage of the Boston Marathon bombings of April 15, 2013. I was on my couch that race day, although most years have found me along the route, cheering (but not running) with thousands of other Bostonians. I have always found marathon Monday to be uniquely uplifting, although the bombings have imbued the occasion with a measure of pathos. One of my friends nervously sheltered in his apartment that night as police pursued the armed suspects in his neighborhood, and a student of mine had been close to the site of explosion earlier in the day. The incident hit close to home.

Having experienced the sorrow of that time period, then, it was sobering to discover the results of a study performed by Lamar Pierce, Todd Rogers, and Jason Snyder.[3] The researchers found that Republicans' sadness over the loss of the 2012 presidential election was actually greater than the sadness experienced by Boston residents in the wake of the marathon bombing. The pain of the election was more acute, too, than the grief felt by parents in the general public after the Sandy Hook elementary school massacre of 2012. If politics is merely sport, it is a sport that exacts a high emotional toll on its spectators.

Given the emotional stakes of politics, it is easy to see how interactions between political tribes can be hindered by emotional responses. There is safety in groups, so from an evolutionary perspective we benefit from mechanisms that nudge us toward group membership. Oxytocin, a feel-good chemical, says Jonathan Haidt, helps bind us to our tribe. And, since danger has lurked outside the tribe throughout our evolutionary experience, we are equipped with an automatic "fight-or-flight" response— no rational, conscious thinking required—to protect ourselves. In the face of danger, the autopilot takes over, cutting off the parts of our brain that deal with reasoning and activating physiological responses like a raised heart rate to fuel an escape.

These days, we don't need a tiger to trigger such a response. "[A]s human lives have grown more complex and multi-faceted, we still often default to very simplistic fight, flight, or freeze reactions during conflicts in our everyday lives," writes Zaid Jilani.[4] According to Theresa Frisbie, an expert in dispute resolution, there is little difference between the brain's perception of a physical and a social threat.[5] A sudden, clarifying jolt of adrenaline feels the same whether triggered by a near miss on the highway or an intolerable tweet.

Just as emotion can mobilize (or immobilize) us to address an immediate threat, so too can it immunize us against longer-lasting damage—such as unwelcome information that could make us doubt ourselves. Jonas Kaplan, Sarah Gimbel, and Sam Harris conducted an experiment to measure the brain activity of people confronted with information that contradicted their deeply held beliefs.[6] Subjects were placed in functional MRI scanners and shown a series of counterarguments to statements with which they strongly agreed. They were then asked to indicate the extent to which they had changed their minds; had the counterarguments convinced them at all? Those people who were most resistant to belief change showed activity in the brain's insular cortex and amygdala, regions that handle emotional reactions. Since the amygdala is activated by threat, the authors suspect that the body may perceive a challenge to deeply held beliefs—a threat to one's very identity—as indistinguishable from a threat to physical safety. When we are confronted with information that contests our understanding of the world, our brains rely on automatic, emotional processes. The rider may have little to do with it.

We enter into the bridge-building business, then, at an evolutionary disadvantage: we are programmed to seek safety in the group, and automatic emotional responses insulate us from the danger that lurks beyond—whether that danger is real or perceived. As Liliana Mason writes, "Our emotional relationships with our opponents must be addressed before we can hope to make the important policy compromises that are required for governing."[7] We must promote in our students the social and emotional dexterity demanded by our times.

Social Emotional Learning

A solution may be social emotional learning. SEL posits that the most successful learning happens in concert with self-awareness and self-management as well as social awareness and relationship skills. For those in the business of education, SEL is nothing new, and its efficacy has been settled. "The promotion of social, emotional, and academic learning is not a shifting educational fad," according to a 2018 Aspen Institute report. "[I]t is the substance of education itself. It is not a distraction from the 'real work' of math and English instruction; it is how instruction can succeed."[8] Conveniently, what we already know to be good educational practice will also move us toward depolarization.

One way SEL can assist in building the skills required to depolarize is by helping students manage their emotional response in the face of challenge. In 1995 Daniel Goleman described the amygdala hijack[9] that happens when our brain, perceiving a threat where none exists, kicks into fight-or-flight mode, immobilizing our ability to rationalize; it's the "freezing" in the face of the MAGA hat for the worried teacher in my workshop. As Jonathan Haidt says, though, someone who weathers the initial flush of the emotional reaction leaves room for the rider—reasoning—to reassert itself. Mindful breathing helps us "hit the brake" on our stress response, for example, allowing us to regain our wits in the face of an emotional surge.[10] This is part of self-management, defined by the Collaborative for Academic, Social, and Emotional Learning (CASEL) as "the abilities to manage one's emotions, thoughts, and behaviors effectively in different situations and to achieve goals and aspirations."[11] If we as a country aspire to transcend our paralysis of polarization, our students must discover that reaching across lines of difference includes a healthy measure of self-awareness and self-management.

Perspective-Taking

But it will also require a more refined social awareness. It is commonplace to hear that we need to take the perspective of those with whom we disagree. The Greater Good Science Center recommends perspective-taking as an effective depolarization strategy,[12] and every school I have ever encountered has in some fashion encouraged students to consider others' perspectives. It turns out, though, that we humans are not always skillful at discerning the intentions or perceptions of others—especially when we are involved.

If polarization is a fire, we in the United States have found plenty of fuel for the blaze. One of those combustibles is indignation—we are disgusted by the disregard "those people" have for us. Researchers have shown, though, that this perception—that we are held in contempt by the political other—is overblown. Just as we are not very good at predicting how our political opposites feel about issues, we also seem to misread how they feel about us. According to recent research, both Republicans and Democrats overestimate the antagonism felt toward them by the political other by a factor of two;[13] the other side does not find us nearly as disagreeable as we think they do. The effect has also been shown to hold for people's perception of how their political party (as opposed to themselves as individuals) is perceived, with further polarization a predictable consequence of this misperception. As researchers Jeffrey Lees and Mina Cikara put it, "When group leaders and other group members believe that the out-group will react with animosity and perceive one's group in a highly negative fashion, they are likely to support antagonistic intergroup actions over cooperative and reconciliatory behaviours."[14] People simply are not very cooperative when they think the other side is out to get them. This is an issue of inaccurate meta-perception—the understanding of how one is perceived by others.

Lees and Cikara offer a solution, which is to correct the misperception. This is perhaps a simple matter in the laboratory of a social scientist, where researchers can quickly transmit to study participants the relevant data that would help them reappraise the situation and modify their perceptions accordingly. But cultivating the habits that will lead people to habitually strive to understand how people across the political aisle really view them will require sustained practice. This is the social awareness element of SEL: "The abilities to understand the perspectives of and empathize with others, including those of different backgrounds, cultures, and contexts."[15] For most people, training is required.

The field of SEL provides a blueprint to implement that training, and, according to education professor Hunter Gehlbach, perspective-taking lies at the heart of SEL work. "[A]t the core of SEL—after one peels away the surrounding layers— lies a single, teachable capacity that anchors almost all of our social interactions: social perspective taking, or the capacity to make sense of others' thoughts and feelings."[16] According to Gehlbach, effective perspective-taking is comprised of four discrete steps.

The first is simply wanting to do it. Shortly after the 2016 presidential election, I spoke with an anguished colleague, who told me, "I just wish I could talk to one Trump voter. I need to understand." That's how the perspective-taking journey starts— by finding the motivation to do it. The second step, according to Gehlbach, is to follow a perspective-taking strategy that fits the situation. A fearless public speaker might not understand the anxiety of a friend living with the dread of delivering a wedding toast. Instead, conjuring up one's own authentic fears—being stuck in an elevator, for example—might be more effective. Step three is to pay attention to the right data. There's no point in trying to read someone's body language, says Gehlbach, if you're talking to them on the phone. Finally, we must work hard to figure out if we are on track—if our inferences about another person's perspective appear to be accurate.

I know from experience that students do not naturally take these steps on their own. Text-based communication (social media posts, emails, texts) particularly exposes their interpersonal immaturity. Kids often fail to anticipate the impact of their words, and they can be wildly off base when interpreting the meaning of the messages they receive; in Gehlbach's parlance, they misread the data. But that's what we educators are for; we can make an impact.

To do so, Gehlbach offers three pieces of advice. First, he encourages teachers to habitually invite multiple perspectives. This can even be as simple, he says, as inviting several students to offer their thoughts on complex issues. Secondly, Gehlbach suggests encouraging students to be social detectives, rather than social judges, by wondering "Why did he say that?" or "What's her side of the story?" Finally, he advises teachers to provide regular feedback to their students as they practice their social-detective skills. In short, perspective-taking, according to Gehlbach, includes discrete steps that, like many skills, require thoughtful instruction and ample practice.

Marc Brackett, the founder and director of the Yale Center for Emotional Intelligence, considers perspective-taking to be enabled by self-regulation, which itself requires the foundational skills of recognizing, understanding, labeling, and expressing emotions.[17] Brackett suggests employing cognitive reframing— also known as reappraisal—as a way to gain perspective, which might include reconsidering what triggered an emotional response in order to defuse the initial charge of emotion in the face of challenge. My takeaway after reading Brackett's book, *Permission to Feel*, is that our sometimes simplistic solutions to polarization (*You should just try to see his perspective*) discount the degree of social and emotional maturity required to implement them. It is possible to get kids to see things from a different point of view, but merely wishing it to happen is not sufficient. The pathway to "seeing the other side" passes through social and emotional learning.

And social emotional learning is increasingly intertwined with media literacy, as the heated emotions sparked by our political, tribal conflicts have become a familiar feature of our media ecospheres. To take seriously the role of emotions, then, is to also consider media's place in our national divide and guide students toward a healthier relationship with that media.

Media Literacy

In 2016, Edgar Maddison Welch drove to Washington, DC to liberate children he believed had been forced into an underage sex ring by presidential candidate Hillary Clinton. As he did so, he was overcome by the emotion born of righteous opposition to the political other, his "heart breaking," he later said, "over the thought of innocent people suffering."[18] When Welch stormed into the Comet pizza restaurant, automatic rifle in hand, his misplaced activism hammered home an unavoidable point: that "fake news" had become serious business. According to a Rolling Stone article, in the days before Welch traveled from his home in North Carolina to Washington, his media diet had included InfoWars videos in which host Alex Jones warned listeners of the satanic rituals Clinton was leading in the pizza joint's basement.[19]

The previous year, the United States Army had planned an elaborate training exercise known as Jade Helm 15, in response to which Jones posted the headline "feds preparing to invade Texas."[20] This set off a snowballing conspiracy theory about the federal government's imminent plan to subdue and occupy parts of the American Southwest. I discovered Jones, InfoWars, and the Jade Helm frenzy while planning a class on the Second Amendment, and, as my students and I watched videos of heavily armed Texans preparing to fight the federal government, we discussed "well-regulated militias" and the media messaging that was fueling their growth. Emotions were running high.

As a social studies teacher, I have always encouraged my students to interrogate their sources; this is part and parcel of teaching social studies. But the internet age has blown the doors off the structures that used to contain information. Renee Hobbs laid out the challenge in a 2017 paper:[21]

> So-called "fake news" is rising in visibility and influence due to the *attention economy*, a concept first developed by Herbert A. Simon in 1971. Many choices are available to us as both consumers and creators of media, and, sadly, it seems as if people have adopted a problematic post-truth

attitude: If it's entertaining or meshes with their own views, who really cares if it's true? This makes it easy for creators of "fake news" in a world where digital content is cheap to produce. These sites use sensationalism (sex, violence, children, animals, and the mysterious unknown) to profit from viral sharing, where more clicks equals more revenue. And when articles include emotionally inflamed or intense words or images, they spread quickly and reach a larger audience.

In the time since Hobbs wrote that article, the term "fake news" has itself become politicized. As employed by Hobbs, the expression indicates sensational misinformation or outright lies, while former President Trump frequently employed the term as a jab against what he deemed unfair treatment at the hands of mainstream media. The phrase itself, then, is as divisive as the content it describes, emblematic of the chasm that has opened up in our polarized battle to report the world as we see it.

We humans gravitate toward information that affirms our beliefs[22] and avoid information that challenges them, which is known in social psychology as "selective exposure."[23] We tune in to what *feels* right, and, thanks to the internet, we have constructed for ourselves comfy "pillow forts of information"[24] that insulate us and exacerbate our divisions. A quick self-inventory will reveal for most people which news sources affirm our worldviews and which threaten them, and academic studies prove what most of us already know: we get our news from CNN or Fox, but rarely from both.[25]

The media business model aids and abets our instinctive search for information that affirms our worldviews. Even before the internet took over, newspapers catered to the political leanings of their readers. According to Bill Bishop, in areas of strong Republican presence newspapers have been found to lean right in their political coverage, while those in Democratic zip codes lean left.[26] Nowadays, media is engaged in "an all-out war for the time of an audience that has more choices than at any time in history,"[27] according to Ezra Klein. TV news personalities hew towards the provocative in the interest of ratings, and the masters of social media leverage our fears. "Growing and keeping people interested in a political social media account," says Senator Ben Sasse, "…[is] simply a matter of capitalizing on the outrage feedback loop: spot something stupid an obscure liberal/conservative said; use it to malign all liberals/conservatives; watch your profile rise as you become a hero to people on your side and a villain to people on the opposite side; rinse and repeat."[28] He calls this "nutpicking."

Surrounded in our digital worlds by people who agree with us, the distance between us and the political "other" grows, and the more news we consume, the greater our polarization. "[R]ather than making Americans more informed," says More in Common, "media coverage is now feeding our misperceptions."[29] Severed from cross-cutting conversation in our social-media bubbles, we observe the "nuts" from afar, with incivility in the opposing tribe's media further repelling us.[30] As we turn inward, absorbing the messaging of like-minded confederates within our media spheres, we grow more extreme in our own positions, a well-documented result, according to Bill Bishop, of surrounding oneself with like-minded thinking.[31]

Psychology primes us to seek safety in an affirming media ecosystem, and the business model of media capitalizes on that instinct, showering us with material to stoke our fears of the "other" and to reassure us of the virtuousness of our tribes. Whether because of the spread of misinformation or the mischaracterizations that come from embedding ourselves in our own media bunkers, it feels very much as if we Americans have lost a collective grip on a shared factual reality. Our understanding of our political opposites fades with distance, and facts themselves feel subjective. This worries former President Obama. "If we do not have the capacity to distinguish what's true from what's false, then by definition the marketplace of ideas doesn't work. And by definition our democracy doesn't work. We are entering into an epistemological crisis."[32] It's hard to know what's real anymore.

Black Confederates

Several years ago, I stumbled onto a YouTube video entitled "A Tribute to Our Black Confederate Heroes"[33] that challenged my students to discern fact from fiction. The video featured grainy photos of African Americans, some of whom wore what appeared to be medals around their necks. The Confederate battle flag appeared in several frames. Complementing this imagery was a bluesy song about an enslaved man who fought lustily alongside Confederate soldiers in defense of Dixie. Overall, the video painted the picture of forgotten Black Confederates who resisted the Union army, leaving the viewer to infer that the Confederate cause—and the flag that symbolizes it—was a struggle against tyranny rather than the preservation of slavery. Because, come on, if Black people were fighting for the Confederacy, how could it be otherwise?

Kids loved the video. The photos intrigued them, and the song was irresistible. After a couple of passes, they were believers. These men, students surmised, were Confederate soldiers—you could tell because they had medals. Also, the pictures looked old, and the Civil War happened a long time ago. The song was captivating. I would ask students to note the passages that stood out. The narrator, they recalled, spoke of the kindness of his master and the wrenching sadness of seeing him killed in battle. *Yes*, I would tell my students. *I heard that too! What else?* "Well, at the end it basically says that black is just another version of rebel gray—like the gray Confederate uniforms." *Ah. I see.* "Like, stop paying so much attention to skin color, because they were all fighting together for what they believed in."

It took about a full class period to digest the visuals, to listen to the song a couple of times, to discuss the words, to watch again after taking note of other students' observations, at which point everyone in the class would be thoroughly convinced that I had been holding out on them: the war wasn't just about slavery. Knowing that Black people fought for the Confederacy, it couldn't have been. And this Confederate flag—the focus of our mock Supreme Court hearing and the subject of discussions with students in Alabama—had a bit more shine to it now; maybe this was a more gallant symbol than we had imagined.

On day two, as I coaxed students to adopt a more critical mindset, that story crumbled. *What are the names of these people who appear in the photographs? What do you know about them? These medals—what are they? And why are some of the photos actually of the same guy?* "Whoa!" students would exclaim. "I didn't notice that!" *Let's revisit the song. The narrator killed how many people?* "A dozen." *And how did he do that?* "The song says he did it with his bare hands." *Ah yes. And then what? What did he do next?* "And then he killed another 12 Union soldiers." *Why? Why did he kill 24 people with his bare hands?* "Because he was really mad that his master had been killed." *Right. He was irate—blinded by rage, whipped into a killing frenzy—because the person who had enslaved him had fallen in battle.* There would always be a moment of silence. *Did that really make sense?* Students would admit that, upon reflection, it did rather stretch the limits of credibility.

The coup de grace would come in the form of the one picture about which we could actually learn anything concrete. Labeled "1st Louisiana Native Guard," the photo shows a lineup of African Americans who, any viewer might assume, fought for the Confederacy. In fact, the remainder of the lesson revealed the photo to have been a doctored and relabeled version of one taken of Union soldiers.[34] Subject to scrutiny, the video lost its credibility, layer by layer, paving the way for students to learn that the legend of the "Black Confederate" is essentially a myth; few African Americans fought for the Confederacy, and those who did in the final, hopeless weeks were forced to. Consequently, the implication that the Civil War was fought for reasons other than the defense of slavery withered under the classroom microscope.

The central question we considered would guide the scrutiny of any piece of media: *Who made this video, and why?* Many of my students struggled to distinguish the narrator of the song from the author of the lyrics. *What do you know about the person who wrote the song?* "Well, we know he killed a bunch of people…" *Really? Do we know the event actually happened?* That the author and narrator could be two distinct entities—and that the implausible events of the song may in fact have been fiction—was a conceptual reach for many of my students. It was an important one, though, worth spending a class period or two discussing, even at the expense of "covering" a couple of Civil War battles. We could find no concrete answers as to who created the video or who wrote or performed the song, although we all got the drift eventually—that this uncertainty about authorship called into question the credibility of the video's message. But we really had to *work* to get there.

The documentary *The Social Dilemma* employs the image of a lifeless body being physically manipulated by the technology giants who, the film suggests, drive our behavior. Despite being a little creepy—or maybe because of it—the image resonates. In countless ways, we increasingly defer to technology: I let my phone correct my texts; I receive an email, and Google offers to respond for me; I open a web browser and a dozen news stories have been curated especially for me; YouTube steers me (and Edgar Maddison Welch) toward content that echoes whatever I have already watched; my students research, and the online service that auto-formats their bibliographies even tells them if a source contains bias—no thinking required!

Media literacy is meant to immunize against—or at least minimize—that manipulation. According to the National Association for Media Literacy Education (NAMLE), a broad conceptualization of media literacy includes "active inquiry and critical thinking about the messages we receive and create so as to develop informed, reflective, and engaged participants essential to a democratic society."[35] Media literacy encourages agency, inviting students to ask questions about authorship and audience (*Who made this? Who paid for it? Who is the intended audience?*), messages and meanings (*What does this want me to think? What's being left out?*), and reality (*Is this fact, opinion, or something else? How credible is this?*).[36]

In other words, a purposeful media literacy program inspires students to ask the very questions overlooked by those who follow online conspiracy theorists such as Alex Jones. "If schools are to fulfill their social purpose of preparing students for life in a democratic society," says Renee Hobbs, "education leaders will need to get creative about how to ensure students are thoughtful and intelligent about the information they consume, and that in the face of increasing polarization, they can tell the fake from the facts."[37] Effective media literacy programs do this. Studies show that media literacy programs help people distinguish between claims that are based in evidence and those that lack standing.[38] Says Patrick Nyhan, "[E]ven brief exposure to interventions that provide guidelines and recommendations for identifying accurate information can reduce belief in false claims and help people distinguish between false and mainstream news."[39] The programming works, and any serious commitment to depolarization requires that we engage in it meaningfully with our students.

Implementing SEL and Media Literacy in the Classroom

That meaningful engagement requires commitment among all teachers, not just a handful of technology specialists who assume the burden of boosting digital citizenship. "Media literacy is doomed to fail if it is a separate, standalone course," says Joel Breakstone, Director of the Stanford History Education Group. "If it is a barnacle on the hull of a bloated curriculum, it's going to be scraped off when there is a crisis or budget crunch."[40] Consequently, teachers should sniff out resources and activities they can integrate into daily teaching. Common Sense Media has an array of resources, searchable by grade level, in its Digital Citizenship Curriculum that fit the bill.[41] NAMLE, too, provides links to numerous curricular materials that support the development of healthy media literacy skills among students. It is easy to imagine, for example, how teachers might introduce even young students to key concepts (*watch out for "Scary Share-y," who unwittingly aids in the spread of misinformation!*[42]) early in a school year and then revisit those concepts as the year unfolds.

Among the questions embedded in NAMLE's conceptualization of media literacy, one cuts to the heart of our national polarization: "*How does this make me feel and how do my emotions influence my interpretation of this?*" Our understanding of media—and indeed our perception of the political "other"—is inextricably linked with emotions. And emotions are intertwined with our social and intellectual selves. As Dr. Robert Jagers, CASEL's Vice President of Research, puts it, "Learning is a relational process. We are not simply cognitive. We are not simply emotional. We are not simply social. We are all those things simultaneously."[43] To that end, social emotional learning, like media literacy, should be featured throughout a child's educational experience, "integrated," according to CASEL, "throughout all classrooms with a systemic, schoolwide approach."[44]

One section of Common Sense's Digital Life Resource Center is devoted specifically to linking media literacy to social emotional standards, promising to "support your students' social and emotional learning as they navigate the digital world."[45] Organized into lessons for elementary, middle, and high school students, examples include "My Feelings When Using Technology" to promote self-awareness among lower-schoolers and "Saying Goodbye to Technology" to help our youngest students regulate their emotions when screen time is finished. Middle school lessons include "Dealing with Digital Drama" to build social awareness, while high schoolers find more sophisticated material, such as "The Impacts of Hate Speech."

Like Common Sense, CASEL is an indispensable resource for SEL programming, and their *SEL 3 Signature Practices Playbook* provides one-stop shopping for a range of SEL activities to be painlessly incorporated into daily lessons across grades and disciplines.[46] The first of the three signature practices is called "welcoming inclusion activities," which can be as simple (and profound) as establishing a daily routine of greeting each child at the classroom door. "The more we fully share ourselves and are fully received and understood by others," reads the guide, "the stronger and safer our learning environments become."[47] In a "What's New" activity, each student briefly shares some personal news, while "Mix and Mingle," introduced to me by my friend and colleague, C.J. Bell, and featured in this section of the guide, has kids mill about the classroom until given the signal to grab the nearest human and chat; the conversation prompt might be innocuous (*Who's your favorite superhero?*) or more personal (*What are you looking forward to*?). This was always a crowd-pleasing activity in my classroom, an efficient mechanism to revive tired bodies and spark interpersonal exchanges.

The second practice in CASEL's guide is referred to as "engaging activities." They "embed brief and relevant experiences that engage participants emotionally throughout content delivery, to better ensure that concepts transfer into long-term memory."[48] The nature of these activities varies widely, from those that help students transition from one task to another (such as using an "attention signal" like a bell) to those that help reinforce the content of the lesson. In "Give One, Get One, Move On," for example, students jot down a few key takeaways from their recent learning experience before sharing one with a partner, receiving one from that partner, and then moving on to repeat the process with someone else. A brain break, in which students take a mindful minute to focus on breathing, is another example of these "engaging activities."

"Optimistic Closure" constitutes the third and final set of activities in the CASEL guide. These activities may be reflective in nature, they may encourage students to anticipate what comes next, or they may spark connections to other work. One example is the "human bar graph," in which students assemble in the line that best represents their current level of understanding. Another activity asks students to share with a partner one thing they're curious about at the end of a lesson, while a "one-word whip around" gives every child a chance to share the single word that expresses how they feel or what they learned that day.

Conclusion: Here's How Not to Behave

If teachers doubt the need to lay a sturdy foundation of social emotional learning and media literacy for students, they should consider our elected officials, whose disfunction provides a cautionary tale about the perils of devaluing healthy social interaction and leveraging emotional triggers for political gain.

Years ago, fresh from college, I spent several months as an intern in the office of Senator John Kerry, a Democrat from

Massachusetts. Although my days were generally filled with tedious tasks performed alongside other lowly staffers, I recall one bright spot: enjoying a beer with Senator Alan Simpson, Republican from Wyoming, who had joined the office holiday party. It was exciting, I admit, to meet the power brokers of Washington, D.C., who themselves seemed to rub shoulders with each other across party lines.

Rarely any longer does this happen. Decades ago, many members of Congress lived full-time with their families in Washington, and their familiarity with each other cultivated a degree of civility. "It's difficult to call somebody a nasty name when your kid and their kid are in the cub scouts together," observed Congressman Emanuel Cleaver about that bygone era.[49] These days, members race back to their home states after each truncated legislative work week to beat the fundraising bushes, leaving little time for socializing across party lines. Even when members of Congress are in the same room, they stick to their tribes. A demoralizing 2019 study used C-SPAN video footage to document that our leaders' failure to cross the aisle is not just metaphorical; increasingly, members of Congress literally remain on their sides of the legislative chamber, eschewing the cross-cutting conversations that once helped grease the wheels of bipartisanship.[50]

As our political leaders have moved away from cross-cutting social outreach, they have corralled voters with emotional triggers, and none more masterfully than Donald Trump. Arlie Hochschild, author of *Strangers in their Own Land*, lived off and on for several years among far-right residents of southern Louisiana, and she was on hand to witness Trump's presidential campaign in 2016. "Trump is an 'emotions candidate,'" wrote Hochschild. "More than any other presidential candidate in decades, Trump focuses on eliciting and praising emotional responses from his fans rather than on detailed policy prescriptions. His speeches— evoking dominance, bravado, clarity, national pride, and personal uplift—inspire an emotional transformation."[51]

In addition to rallying the faithful, politicians leverage emotion to demonize the political "other." William Brady and colleagues have studied politicians' use of social media to amplify their messaging and influence, finding that the use of moral-emotional language fuels the most effective message dispersion. For presidential candidates and sitting members of congress, the key is to hit the public's deepest moral-emotional buttons. Words like "blamed," "brutal," and "hurt" appeared in Donald Trump's most retweeted posts before the 2016 election, while language such as "compassion," "defense," and "hell" fueled Hillary Clinton's retweets. The researchers found that moral anger provided particularly effective fuel for message dispersion, noting that anger "increases opinion confirmation;"[52] angry people *know* they're right. Politicians have learned how to leverage our automatic, emotional responses to group threat, and modern media abets their efforts.

Our political leaders' misconduct, as frustrating as it may be, serves to remind us educators of our mandate. As elected officials decreasingly engage across the aisle, we must help students sharpen their social awareness and relationship skills. As politicians leverage emotions for political gain, we must bolster the emotional literacy among our students that will fortify them against these tactics. It is our job to help students take control of their media, rather than allow themselves to be controlled—particularly through emotional manipulation—by it.

But if we're being honest, we educators are every bit as susceptible to emotional manipulation and media illiteracy as our students. As we think about how to guide them, then, it is unavoidable that we face up to the work we, ourselves, must do, which is the subject of Chapter Seven.

Notes

1   Berardino, 2012
2   Haidt, 2012
3   Pierce et al., 2015
4   Jilani, 2019
5   Jilani, 2019
6   Kaplan et al., 2016
7   Mason, 2018, p. 101

8   The Aspen Institute, 2018, p. 6
9   Goleman, 1995
10 Brackett, 2019
11 CASEL, 2022 "What Is the CASEL Framework?"
12 Shigeoka & Marsh, 2020
13 Moore-Berg et al., 2020
14 Lees & Cikara, 2020
15 CASEL, 2022 "What Is the CASEL Framework?"
16 Gehlbach, 2017, p. 10
17 Brackett, 2019
18 Goldman, 2016
19 Robb, 2017
20 Baddour, 2015
21 Hobbs, 2017, p. 26
22 Hart et al., 2009
23 Iyengar & Hahn, 2009
24 Beck, 2017
25 Iyengar & Hahn, 2009
26 Bishop, 2008, p. 301
27 Klein, 2020, p. 140
28 Sasse, 2018, p. 110
29 More in Common, 2019
30 Druckman et al., 2019
31 Bishop, 2008, p. 67
32 Goldberg, 2020
33 Heritage Not Hate Productions, 2007
34 Handler & Tuite, 2009
35 National Association for Media Literacy Education, 2001
36 Rogow & Scheibe
37 Hobbs, 2017, p. 31
38 Kahne & Bowyer, 2017
39 Nyhan, 2020, p. 230
40 Collins, 2021
41 Common Sense Media "Digital Citizenship Curriculum"
42 National Association for Media Literacy Education, 2021
43 CASEL, 2022 "Advancing Social and Emotional Learning"
44 CASEL, 2022 "SEL in the Classroom"
45 Common Sense Media "SEL in Digital Life Resource Center"

46 CASEL, 2019
47 CASEL, 2019, p. 10
48 CASEL, 2019, p. 19
49 Langhorne, 2018
50 Merrefield, 2019
51 Hochschild, 2016, p. 225
52 Brady et al., 2019, p. 1811

7

Positioning Faculty to Encourage Depolarization

"Hey, Mr. Lenci, want to hear a political joke?" Recess ended, and seventh graders arrived in a gust of Goldfish crumbs and cold air. "Allie," armed with her backpack and a sense of humor, bounced on her feet in anticipation. "So, you're ready for the political joke?" I was. "Wait for it...DONALD TRUMP!"

At the time—it must have been the winter of 2016, with the Republican convention still many months away—Donald Trump *was* a political joke among Democrats as well as the Republican establishment, and here was a student of mine, all 12 years of age, piling it on. I was flooded with questions: *Do I laugh this off? Is there a threshold of political gravitas for a candidate to reach, at which point joking becomes political commentary? Has Trump reached that level? What will other students read into my response? Are there any Goldfish left?*

I think often of that moment. Intuition led me to affirm the jokester ("clever!") and move on without making a stink. But what a difference a year would have made. At what moment did Donald Trump transition from business mogul/reality-show celebrity to legitimate political figure? Once that transition occurred, did new rules of engagement apply to discussing him in school? Was his behavior as a private citizen open to critique in the classroom (in the same way a sports star might be)? Were students and/or

DOI: 10.4324/9781003289494-7

faculty then prohibited from commenting on his behavior once he had passed into the realm of the "political?" More broadly, what are the guardrails for dialogue across lines of difference in schools?

For teachers who accept the thesis that students must reach across ideological lines if they are to grow into a high-functioning citizenry, we adults have our own work to do, our own questions to answer. A school that values this work must engage in thoughtful professional development that includes training and introspection on the part of individual teachers. We educators are products of and participants in the same polarized society that awaits our students. We occupy political echo chambers and rely on one-sided media like everyone else, and we carry our political allegiances into the classroom. No playbook reminds us what to say when our 12-year-old student makes a joke out of the future president of the United States; we need to work on this.

Educators' Media Consumption

That work begins with an examination of the media we consume. In my little corner of coastal Massachusetts, most of my colleagues draw from the same wells: the *New York Times*, CNN, *The Atlantic*, *Vox*, the *Huffington Post* and other left-leaning news outlets. Until recently, I did too. But I've attempted to practice what I preach by switching things up. I ditched the *New York Times*, accepted the "low, introductory rate" offered by the *Wall Street Journal*, and downloaded the Read Across The Aisle app—a service that gathers news from across the political spectrum and monitors the user's choice of media outlets.[1] I'll be honest: for weeks after abandoning the *Times*, I felt disoriented and untethered. I struggled to calibrate the importance of headlines. Was this story in *The Hill* the real news of the day? How far down the homepage would it have appeared in the *Times*? Did this Reuters newsfeed include everything I really needed to know? Was I missing something important?

In his book, *Them: Why We Hate Each Other—and How to Heal*, Senator Ben Sasse shares a tale of media bias.[2] In 2013, Kermit Gosnell went on trial. Gosnell was a Philadelphia physician who, according to investigators, performed gruesome late-term abortions in collaboration with unlicensed staff in a facility that reminded one agent of a "bad gas station restroom."[3] But no one paid much attention. The *Washington Post* ignored the trial completely, according to journalist Kirsten Powers, while the *New York Times* buried a single story on its 17th page.[4]

Writing in Bloomberg, the journalist Geoffrey Goldberg discussed why this was so. He recalled his own, earlier coverage of Planned Parenthood's loss of funding, a move that set off alarm bells among pro-choice Americans. "Where is that same assiduousness on the Gosnell case," he asked, "a case that shocks the conscience?"[5] Powers added, "Let me state the obvious. This should be headline news."[6] That it was not, according to Senator Sasse, reflected what he considers to have been a misguided attempt to quiet a story that would have challenged a pro-choice bias in the national media. In other words, Sasse contends—and, in retrospect, journalists agree—that the media buried a story that did not fit the left-leaning mold.

Even suggesting that mainstream media has a liberal bias is likely to feel prickly to most progressive teachers, because it triggers tribal allegiances. President Trump was relentlessly dismissive of and at times abusive toward journalists during his presidency, and the defense of a free press in opposition to him animated progressives. To contend that the *Washington Post* or the *New York Times* ever blew it, then, may feel vaguely threatening to those whose political identity was sharpened in opposition to President Trump. During an online workshop in 2020, a head of school wrote to me in the chat bar, "I take a peek at Fox news every day just to see what they're saying, and everyone thinks I'm crazy." It is deceivingly difficult to move out of our media comfort zone. We grow disoriented. And part of that disorientation stems from what can almost be perceived as disloyalty: *Wait, that guy watches Fox News now?* Nonetheless, a teacher who intends to help students understand bias and who earnestly wishes for them to appreciate different points of view must consider that his or her own sources of information almost certainly include blind spots.

A number of tools can help us diversify our news consumption. AllSides provides a range of media sources for every major story of the day, while the Flip Side focuses on a single event and packages news snippets from across the political spectrum.

Ground News has an interesting feature called "Blindspot" that flags stories being covered exclusively or heavily by media from just one side of the political spectrum. The journalist Isaac Saul publishes a newsletter, Tangle, that aggregates reporting from both sides of the aisle, as well as Saul's commentary on that reporting. If we genuinely wish for students to be curious about the media they consume, we must bring the same spirit of open-mindedness to our own news intake.

We must, however, do more than just model a healthy relationship with media. We also need to model healthy relationships with each other. Our attempts to engineer cross-cutting conversations in the classroom or to partner students with their counterparts in other classrooms will only be as successful as our own willingness to practice the same bridge-building skills with each other.

Faculty Members Talking Across the Political Divide

A couple of months before the 2020 presidential election, when the national atmosphere could not have been much more tense, one of my workshops included the hypothetical scenario mentioned in Chapter Six:

> It's November 2020. President Trump has won reelection. A jubilant student comes to school wearing a MAGA hat, although hats are prohibited by the school's dress code. You are feeling personally vulnerable at this moment, and the hat triggers a visceral response within you. You feel paralyzed by the sight of it. How, if at all, do you engage the child?

Teachers were anguished at the prospect of a Trump victory, and the word "jubilant" stopped one attendee in her tracks. "Wow," she said. "That would honestly make me wonder if I belonged at that school." For months afterward, I found myself returning to her response and the questions it provoked: What does it mean to belong at a school? Does belonging presuppose agreement? What place, if any, is there for a member of the community who holds viewpoints in opposition to the majority? These were questions, in fact, that I had already begun to consider.

The Massachusetts school that employed me for 14 years is predictably staffed by a preponderance of progressive teachers. But they aren't all left leaning, and during my final year there, I set out to explore the viewpoint diversity that had been generally overlooked in my time at the school. An institutional structure stood ready to house the work: an optional gathering of faculty to discuss a single topic related to diversity in education each year, known by the acronym IDEA. Precedent had established a calendar of roughly six annual meetings, with each session commencing just after students left the building. In 2018 I volunteered to lead an exploration of political differences within the faculty. And then I held my breath.

It went surprisingly well. Each gathering featured a single, brave, conservative faculty member sharing the personal journey that informed his or her political outlook. Through those stories—of childhood, family, and work—we made progress. Tribal barriers shrank as empathy expanded. One evening a presenter discussed his family's cherished plot of land. With this land came challenges that required the use of a rifle. The utility of that rifle was an integral part of operating the land, and the stewardship of the land was a source of pride for the entire family. Gun ownership made sense. I doubt anyone in the room changed their mind about gun control, but for the first time, many in attendance could say they truly understood the motivation of someone who valued the Second Amendment.

Structure was our friend. Following each presenter's initial narrative, we asked clarifying questions. *This is not an invitation to poke holes in the volunteer's story*, read our guidelines. *To the contrary, it is a chance to more deeply understand and appreciate that person's point of view.* When those clarifying questions had been answered, everyone turned to a written reflection: *This section does not ask you to change your mind about anything, just that you record what you've heard.* Finally, we closed each session with a period of verbal reflection, during which attendees thanked the volunteer by showing that they had heard—whether or not they agreed with—what had been shared.

In retrospect, although I relied mostly on intuition to draw up the contours of that experience, research validates the approach (as a former colleague likes to say, "Even a blind squirrel finds a nut once in a while.") According to the Greater Good Science Center, "It turns out that many conditions have to be met for contact to reduce prejudice, including having contact be sustained, with more than one member of the group, including a genuine exchange of ideas...."[7] We nailed those conditions, meeting throughout the year and inviting a range of presenters. The focus on personal stories—as opposed to policy positions—was a good move, affirmed by a recent survey of studies showing that personal narratives more effectively bridge moral and political divides than do facts.[8] Finally, the written reflection acted as a pause button, allowing for the amygdala hijack that Daniel Goleman described to run its course before yielding to reasoning.

Conservatives in the Closet

If I'm being honest, I had the liberals in mind when I designed that professional-development experience. The progressive majority in our school needed practice listening to and building empathy for people with whom they disagreed. The conservatives were the foil, stepping up to perform a service; at least that's the way I designed it. What I had not anticipated was the weight that would be lifted from the backs of those conservative faculty members as they shared their stories. Recall that we are ideologically polarized, but that the more profound divide may be *affective* polarization: we *feel* warmth towards members of the in-group and we *feel* negativity towards members of the out-group. We sustain ourselves through the emotional nourishment of the group, and when we do not feel included, we suffer.

One long-serving and highly respected former colleague experienced this alienation when politics and work collided:

> After the 2016 election, my husband took a job on the presidential transition team. In a split second, almost all of my relationships at school came crumbling down. I was alone. I was a ghost in the hallways. No one wanted

to interact with me. Certainly no one wanted to hear my voice. Trump hysteria had set in.

This teacher's sense of isolation was not at its core ideological—she leaned right on some issues, yet she disagreed with aspects of Trump's approach and proposals. She did not suddenly find herself in acrimonious rows over policy positions. Rather, her sudden estrangement was about *belonging*. It was dizzying to have been securely rooted in her school community for two decades before feeling abruptly cast out. Remember, the students we see clinging desperately to each other as they move uneasily down the hallway eventually become us—or, we have always been them. We do not shed our need for social affirmation when we graduate. Evolution has positioned us to seek group membership and to be mistrustful of the out-group. We teachers occupy positions on either side of the political divide, just like the rest of our fellow citizens.

The bravest among us will recognize that the political sorting within our own faculties presents its challenges but also opportunities. Can a school afford to overlook the fact that a handful of conservative teachers quietly go about their business in otherwise left-leaning communities? Certainly. But if it is serious about positioning students to reach across lines of ideological or political divide, it should start by first exposing faculty to that work.

The realist in me knows that most schools will not quickly leap into the fraught terrain of cross-cutting political conversation among faculty members. In that case, it may make sense for schools to feature others who are doing the work. For several months I have been a card-carrying member of Braver Angels, "a national citizens' movement to bring liberals, conservatives, and others together at the grassroots level, not to find centrist compromise but to find one another as citizens."[9] Through Braver Angels I have witnessed debates on gun control and voting rights among people who disagree but who approach the table in good faith. The experience has helped me more deeply appreciate—without necessarily agreeing with—viewpoints that challenge my own.

Other organizations encourage this work, too. Living Room Conversations ("healing divides starts with conversation"[10]) and the Civic Health Project ("… dedicated to reducing toxic partisan polarization…"[11]) are two examples. Zoom affords a degree of distance and perhaps anonymity that softens the intensity of engaging in dialogue across lines of distance. Sitting in my kitchen, munching on cashews, I can take the Braver Angels debate as seriously as I wish, tuning out when my emotional reservoir runs dry.

It's Not So Hard to Do

While it seems daunting to engage our colleagues—often, our friends—in these matters, it might not be so bad. For months, I've been anxious about a possible root canal. I made the mistake of visiting the website of an endodontist, where I read that root canals are unfairly "associated with a great deal of discomfort." My dread remained intact. During my last visit, my dentist informed me that I "wasn't out of the woods yet," so I live with trepidation about this legendarily barbarous invasion of my cuspids.

According to social psychologists Charles Dorison, Julia Minson, and Todd Rogers, though, we humans tend to overestimate our aversion to all sorts of things— not just root canals, but also engaging with the political "other." Opposing views are not as grating as people anticipate. When people actually engage in discussion across the political divide, it's not the painful ordeal they expected.[12] My experience confirms this finding. "Listening became a gift," said one attendee of our IDEA meetings. "Colleagues left the space excited and invigorated by our exchanges," said another. "I was blown away by the candid stories, and I was so impressed by the atmosphere of respect." And, hyperbolic though it may sound, one conservative faculty member wrote, "I really was close to leaving my job…. I think IDEA saved me." Rather than deflating attendees, our IDEA sessions seemed to have something of a leavening effect.

Resources to Help Faculty Learn About Polarization

For those school communities that simply are not ready to ask adults to engage in cross-cutting conversations—or even to investigate other organizations that facilitate such conversations— it could make sense to ease into this work by examining the challenge of polarization from a detached, intellectual level. The Greater Good Science Center's "Bridging Differences" initiative is an excellent source for pithy and accessible summaries of research into the psychology of in-group favoritism, and a slew of articles, including "Six Techniques to Bridge Differences,"[13] would jumpstart a productive faculty conversation on dialogue across difference. The Pew Research Center is an authoritative source on polarization, and OpenMind has assembled a robust library of videos, essays, and scholarly articles organized by theme, including "Uncover the roots of our differences" and "Explore other worldviews"[14] that could also provide fodder for a faculty discussion.

Films might also do the job. *The Reunited States* is a powerful documentary that exposes our national rift and provides hope for mending it.[15] *Dialogue Lab: America*, referenced in Chapter Five, presents a promising model of face-to-face, cross-cutting political discussion.[16] *For the Common Good* documents a public conflict between Simon Greer and Fox News host Glenn Beck and their one-on-one conversation in search of understanding and closure in its wake.[17] There is no shortage of resources to help us educators understand the challenge of polarization and envision its solutions.

Classroom Strategies

Another doorway into this work could be to attack it from a practical angle—by helping teachers plan the strategies and techniques that will best position them to lead students through difficult dialogue.

One way to do so is to present hypothetical scenarios in which an ideological or political divide insinuates itself into the school community. How do we respond when a student expresses a deeply unpopular point of view? Should a faculty member be permitted to display emblems that could be considered political? How do we handle the parent who bemoans the dearth of conservative resources in a given lesson? What do we do when we are accused of "indoctrination?" Tossing out these types of scenarios virtually guarantees a lively discussion.

A lively discussion is not enough, though, since these gab sessions will inevitably stir up philosophical and practical questions that require responses. Teachers may want to know what the word "political" means in their school (for me, everything is political and trying to avoid "politics" in schools is a fool's errand). Teachers deserve guidance as to whether it's appropriate to share their own political opinions (I am inclined to say "no;" in his essay, "Making a Case For Teacher Political Disclosure," though, Wayne Journell makes a very creditable case as to why teachers *should* share their politics with students.[18]) Teachers will have other questions, as well, and they will undoubtedly fret about what to do when contentious conversations among their students go awry. Some of those concerns can be anticipated:

What if I don't know what to say? Recently a teacher told me that a student had called another a "communist" during a classroom discussion. The teacher was utterly flummoxed—caught off guard, unsure whether this comment was intended (or received) maliciously and flooded with the sorts of questions I found myself juggling when informed by my student that Donald Trump was a joke. *Wait, did that just happen? How am I supposed to respond?* Since emotions can temporarily disable reasoning, I've found it best to buy some time. We don't always need to know how to respond in the moment. We just need to be willing to admit (and model) uncertainty and return to the incident when we've gathered our thoughts, as in, "Huh. I need to think about this one. Let me stick that in the parking lot, to be revisited tomorrow." Often, I find that some space—or a collegial conversation—helps me sort out my response.

What if a child gets wounded? Many teachers worry that a contentious conversation could emotionally wound a child. While I believe that children generally benefit from exposure to ideas with which they do not agree, it is certainly possible for dialogue to move beyond discomfort and into the realm of threat for some children at some times. And we may not even realize it. A simple way to capture those unseen moments is to ask students to complete an "exit ticket" at the end of class with a prompt such as, "Is there anything you'd like me to know about today's discussion?" or "How are you feeling about today's conversation?" I've lined up many one-on-one conversations that way over the years, most of which have been brief, with the buffer of a few class periods having softened what felt threatening in the moment. Some of those conversations have revealed deeper concerns that warranted further communication (sometimes with other adults). If we push our students to engage across lines of difference, we must also be ready to provide the support that will allow those students to process and grow from such exchanges.

What if no one is listening? Sometimes, what might have been a "civil conversation," a "better argument," or "deliberative dialogue" ends up as a train wreck, with kids talking on top of each other, arguing for the sake of argumentation, and refusing to listen. Paradoxically, these are valuable experiences. How would we expect children to navigate their way through comparable turbulence later in life if they haven't done so as students? Instead of refereeing the crossfire, teachers should encourage students to reflect on their interactions and find ways to raise the tenor of discussion. Questions such as *how's this conversation going?* or *what have we learned in the last ten minutes?*[19] get that process started. Asking students how they are feeling in the midst of an unproductive conversation can also get the ship aimed in the right direction. This process works best when norms of behavior have been clearly established (see Chapter Five), so that students can measure the moment against those standards.

Wait. Is this really up for discussion? Some of us have had the unsettling experience of starting out on one discussion path—one that might find reasonable people in sincere disagreement—only to realize that at some point we had wandered into territory that, come to think of it, really should not be up for debate. We blink our eyes to clear the cobwebs, and kids are arguing with each other about whether Donald Trump was actually elected president in 2020—even though there is a factual answer to that question. The prospect of ending up in these situations haunts many teachers and makes them hesitant to expose kids to contentious conversations. They are plagued by the uncertainty of how to handle discussions that seem to have a "right answer."

When there is a right answer, we teachers need to provide it or create the conditions for children to find it themselves. And when we realize we've crossed into that lane, we need to acknowledge it (*Well, check this out: we're now debating a question that has a single answer. I can solve this. Trump lost the election*) and shift back into the lane we intended to travel (*but let's get back to the question of whether you find the voting system fair in this country*).[20] Matters of fact should not be treated as fodder for disagreement.

Conclusion: Teachers First

I do not live in the most politically prejudiced county in the United States. That would be Suffolk County, Massachusetts, home of Boston. But I live next door, and my home county doesn't fare much better. In fact, it ranks in the 99th percentile of the most politically intolerant regions in the nation—this, according to a study reported in *The Atlantic* in 2019.[21] While I would have characterized my hometown as *progressive* rather than *intolerant*, I am reminded of the influential conservative writer, William F. Buckley, Jr., who once observed, "Liberals claim to want to give a hearing to other views, but then are shocked and offended to discover that there are other views."[22]

To position our students to meet the challenge of polarization, teachers need to face the fact that we are a cog in the machinery of polarization. To get there, we have our own homework: readings to review, media sources to vary, bridge-building organizations to discover. And for the truly committed, transformative conversations await within school walls among faculty who may not know each other as well as they once thought. The journey towards depolarization begins in schools, where the work, by necessity, starts with adults. This includes teachers, but it also extends to our interaction with parents, which is the focus of Chapter Eight.

Notes

1   Read Across The Aisle
2   Sasse, 2018
3   Goldberg, 2013
4   Powers, 2013
5   Goldberg, 2013
6   Powers, 2013
7   De-Wit et al., 2019
8   Kubin et al., 2021
9   Braver Angels, 2020
10 Living Room Conversations, 2022
11 Civic Health Project
12 Dorison et al., 2019
13 Smith & Smith, 2021
14 OpenMind "OpenMind Library"
15 Rekhi, 2021
16 Pickett & Lawes, 2022
17 For the Common Good
18 Journell, 2016
19 I picked up this question from Simon Greer during the workshop mentioned in Chapter Five.
20 I have heard human sexuality educator Deborah Roffman refer to "an illegal lane change" when people get mixed up in their verbiage. I might make references to gender expression, for example, when I meant to talk about gender identity. I credit Roffman for the helpful metaphor of a "lane change."
21 Ripley et al., 2019
22 Goodreads

8

Partnering With Parents Across the Political Divide

Many years ago, a good friend and colleague was teaching her sixth-grade math class when she noticed a parent peering in through the classroom windows. This parent was a slender woman, but the birch sapling behind which she was trying to hide provided scant cover. For what felt like an eternity, the mother remained in full view of the teacher and students as she desperately tried to snatch a glimpse of her (now mortified) daughter at school. This is what it feels like to be a parent of a growing child: suddenly, inexplicably, on the outside, trying in vain to look back in.

What we teachers receive as accusations, attacks, criticism, and second-guessing is almost always an expression of parental concern—a deep-seated worry about their kids. Technology has amplified that anxiety in the time I have been teaching, manifested in irate emails to teachers, compulsive texts to children during the school day, and incendiary posts on social media. To make matters worse, we've had ourselves a pandemic; people have been a bit on edge.

Perhaps it should come as no surprise, then, that there would be a mobilization among some parents to reassert control over their children's education. That movement has manifested itself as a backlash against the diversity, equity, and inclusion (DEI) initiatives that have gained traction in many schools and school

DOI: 10.4324/9781003289494-8

systems, the energy of which has bewildered educators. Many teachers are mystified by this opposition to what they consider sincere attempts to execute self-evident goals—to reach all children, to empower all children—but the movement is less puzzling when contextualized within the national landscape.

Recall that accord on climate change (see Chapter Three) would appear to be a matter of factual understanding. Provide more research, goes the thinking, and those who deny the urgency—or even the existence—of climate change will change their tune. In similar fashion, some teachers assume that parents lack the training or knowledge to appreciate the importance of diversity, equity, and inclusion initiatives. Or they are misinformed; they've been told that schools are teaching a "critical race theory" (CRT) that has its roots in high-level academia, when in fact this is not the case. Correct the record, and parents will surely come around.

As research shows, though, increased scientific literacy does not correlate with an increased commitment to curbing climate change because the impasse is about group membership, not scientific understanding. The same holds for the standoff between many parents and schools. This showdown has, like every other matter of consequence, been folded into the polarization that stymies Americans. The current debate over education was ignited in the media and fueled by emotional triggers that established CRT as an existential threat. Threat disables rational thinking and invokes a primal instinct to flee or fight—and the fight is now on. It has become a matter of us versus them.

That is the challenge, but it is also the opportunity. If we wish for students to engage in dialogue across lines of disagreement, and if we believe that faculty need to participate in similar work, it stands to reason that the same exercise must be extended to parents. Our instinct may be to circle the wagons and repel the attacks of those whose opposition to DEI work echoes so loudly in the national media, but this will do nothing to model for students how to have these difficult discussions. We must engage. To do so, we should recall what we know to be true about parents: they are worried about their children. As are we teachers. Fundamentally, we are not at odds. But we will need to surface areas of common ground that have been buried by the scorched earth of political warfare if we are to engage in productive conversation.

Disagreement Over the Curriculum Is Nothing New

Conflict over the curriculum is nothing new. A 2011 report entitled "Contested Curriculum: How Teachers and Citizens View Civics Education"[1] documented disagreement between teachers and the general public about what constitutes worthwhile civic education. According to the report, a strong majority of teachers aim to instill a sense of global citizenship in students, while only a third of American citizens think they should. Roughly three-quarters of teachers find it "absolutely essential" to prioritize teaching tolerance for those who are different, yet only about half of the general public agrees. The general public is more likely than educators to prioritize teaching a love of country, and many of those polled agreed with the statement, "Too many social studies teachers use their classes as a 'soap box' for their personal point of view."

In a 2013 paper, Paula McAvoy and Diana Hess shared an anecdote about that "soap box" concern (now referred to as "indoctrination"). In 2009, President Obama made plans to kick off the school year by speaking at a Virginia school. In response, some parents demanded that their children be excused from attending the speech, while others kept their kids home entirely that day. One parent lamented, "I don't want school turned over to some socialist movement."[2] Despite the fact that the speech was "about as nonpartisan as one could imagine,"[3] to some parents the specter of a political figure presenting himself in the classroom was too much to bear. I myself have received the "soap box" accusation from both sides of the aisle. A parent once complained that I was favoring then-President George W. Bush in my class discussions, and when Barrack Obama took over, I was scolded for my perceived Democratic bias. So I get it: tension has long simmered between some parents and the generally more liberal teachers who educate their children.

An Explosion of Parent Groups

This tension has reached a breaking point, with a host of organizations opposing what they perceive to be a progressive bent in schooling. No Left Turn in Education aims to "expose the radical indoctrination in K-12 education,"[4] and Parents Defending Education is similarly "fighting indoctrination in the classroom."[5] Moms for Liberty, born out of its founders' frustration with a "leftist, liberal social agenda,"[6] was active in 33 states as of early 2022, with a membership of approximately 70,000. Some of the recently formed parent groups fear a loss of educational rigor and emphasize the importance of critical thinking.[7] Others sound the alarm over what they consider divisive topics and lament the discomfort of some white students in a predominantly progressive school culture.[8] These organizations are united in believing that things are not as they should be in school.

The movement has charged into the legislative arena. By early 2022, at least 36 states had introduced bills that would restrict teaching about race or gender.[9] A proposed law in Oklahoma would allow parents to seek damages of up to $10,000 directly from teachers believed to be teaching "critical race theory."[10] Should a New Hampshire bill pass, it would be illegal to present the founding of the United States in a negative light,[11] and Indiana lawmakers pushed for mandatory instruction that "socialism, Marxism, communism, totalitarianism, or similar political systems are incompatible with and in conflict with the principles of freedom upon which the United States was founded."[12] As this book went into production, 14 states had recently passed laws putting limits on critical race theory in schools.

Media Sparks the Movement

Like other elements of our national divide, the seeds of division were sown by our national media. In July of 2020, a conservative activist named Christopher Rufo appeared on Laura Ingraham's Fox News show to discuss the infiltration of critical race theory into federal training programs.[13] Rufo joined Tucker Carlson later that summer to sustain his messaging, calling diversity training within the federal government "an existential threat to the United States."[14] Carlson opened that show with extensive video footage of vandalism and looting, later characterizing the mayhem as a consequence of the diversity training Rufo was exposing.[15] Rufo said, "I am declaring a one-man war against 'critical race theory' in the federal government, and I'm not going to stop these investigations until we can abolish it within our public institutions."[16] His ultimate goal, he tweeted, was "to persuade the President of the United States to issue an executive order banning critical race theory in the federal government."[17]

About one month later, on September 22, 2020, President Trump did so, issuing an executive order to halt any training of federal officials that promoted "offensive and anti-American race and sex stereotyping and scapegoating."[18] On November 2, the day before the presidential election, Trump issued another executive order, this one addressing the teaching of American history. "[M]any students are now taught in school to hate their own country," read the order, "and to believe that the men and women who built it were not heroes, but rather villains."[19] In an extraordinary tweet, Trump then characterized critical race theory as an existential threat: "the greatest threat to western civilization," he wrote.[20]

Since then, the battle cry has echoed widely. According to the *Washington Post*, in 2020, conservative media outlets mentioned critical race theory 132 times. June and July of 2021 saw nearly 2,000 media mentions.[21] "I write to you with a sense of alarm," opens Bill Jacobson in his fundraising appeal for a website that tracks the implementation of diversity initiatives in schools. "Our nation is under attack from within by people and groups who seek to tear down our society."[22] The Moms for Liberty website declares the organization "ready to fight those that stand in the way of liberty" and "dedicated to fighting for the survival of America."[23] The founder of No Left Turn in Education says, "This fight is for our children and our nation."[24] No longer a rational discussion, the issue of race in education has improbably come to represent for some an existential fight to save the country itself.

If the language of those opposed to racial work in schools sounds dire, it is merely in keeping with the emotionally charged tenor that has reigned since President Trump declared CRT to be an existential threat. Recall the work of William Brady and colleagues (see Chapter Six), whose study found that the use of moral-emotional language helps messages spread. From the start of this spat, CRT has been presented by its opponents in contemptuous language evoking disgust. Tucker Carlson called diversity training a "grotesque project"[25] and rhetorically asked Rufo, "Why do we allow this kind of garbage to continue, this poison, at public expense?"[26] Appearing on Fox news, Vivek Ramaswamy, author of *Woke Inc.*, said that "wokeism" is "infecting our schools; it's infecting our culture."[27] President Trump adopted similar wording in his executive order, referring to a "malign ideology" that "threatens to infect core institutions of our country."[28] On Twitter he said, "This is a sickness that cannot be allowed to continue. Please report any sightings so we can quickly extinguish!"[29] Against the backdrop of a pandemic, the language of contagion has had the desired effect.

People now guard closely against infection. The website CriticalRace.org lists the diversity initiatives underway at hundreds of schools and colleges.[30] No Left Turn in Education hopes to install classroom cameras to expose leftist teaching,[31] and Virginia Governor Glenn Youngkin established a tip line to allow residents to report instances of "divisive" teaching.[32] Moms for Liberty aspires to be "an ever vigilant watchdog over every school system in the country."[33] As President Trump hoped, people are indeed on high alert for signs of contamination.

In short, the issue of race in schools has—like so many other matters—triggered an intense defense of group identity. A combustible mixture of emotionally charged media messaging and political posturing has leveraged this topic to reinforce group allegiance in the face of a perceived threat from the outsiders. For many caught in this whirlwind, the issue is no longer about policy but rather self- and group-preservation. As such, it has bypassed the rider; the elephant is in charge.

How Not to Respond to That Parent

Several years ago, I climbed out of bed and opened my laptop to find an email from a concerned parent addressed to the seventh-grade teaching team. She objected to her child being asked, for one week, to record moments in which he noticed the presence of race in his daily life. In my history class, we were studying the Civil Rights Movement. The parent appreciated the historical content of that unit, but she contested the premise of the supplemental exercise—that race continues to impact American society. Before I had even halved my children's grapefruit and poured their juice, I responded to her email. In a single, unassailable paragraph, I defended our teaching team's approach and, having dispatched the enemy without even burning my toast, I later enjoyed a hero's welcome in our seventh-grade team meeting.

But I blew it. In the face of what felt like a threat, I fought. My colleagues and I deluded ourselves into chalking up that exchange as a win, when in fact it was a lost opportunity to hear more about the fears and concerns animating that parent and, eventually, to discover some common understanding that might have positioned us to provide more coherent guidance for her child. All I accomplished in firing off that email was to deepen a divide, and, in retrospect, I realize that as I did so I made an assumption: that my motives were pure, while those of the parent who contacted me were questionable.

This is known as "motivation attribution asymmetry," the focus of a 2014 study that sought to explain impasses across lines of deep divide.[34] In essence, people tend to believe their own group is motivated by love, while others are motivated by something less admirable—such as hatred. In retrospect, it is entirely plausible that I subconsciously assumed I was in the right—that my motivation was untainted, while that parent, perhaps burdened by a hint of racism, was out of line. Today, as we absorb the resistance to the diversity, equity, and inclusion initiatives of schools, we educators may be inclined to similarly defend ourselves and to shelter in the purity of our motivation, while ascribing less valor to the motivation of those who question our efforts. Our only productive path forward, though, is to assume that we share a noble motivation and, on the basis of that assumption, enter into an earnest search for common ground.

Searching for Common Ground Between Teachers and Parent Groups

In the fall of 2021, an organization called Parents Unite presented a conference entitled "Diversity of Thought in K-12 Education," which I later watched through the organization's website. I found myself in disagreement with the central premise that seemed to animate almost all of the speakers, which was that schools' diversity initiatives present a clear and present danger. Presenter after presenter referred to the "fight" and the "battle" for children and for the country, and I felt that in such a battle I must be the enemy. It was, frankly, an unusual experience to immerse myself in thinking that was so dissonant with my own. I had to guard constantly against the instinct to roll my eyes, to doubt, to poke holes in what I was hearing. Instead, I took notes on everything I could construe as common ground between my outlook and the viewpoints of the conference presenters. And, lo and behold, I actually found quite a bit.

Freedom of expression: One of the sharpest themes of the conference was, to my ears, the concern over students self-censoring. There is a widespread belief among some parents that "woke culture" has become the norm in education and that it leaves no room for dissent—that pressure from peers as well as adults suffocates viewpoint diversity. People feel "policed," according to one speaker.[35] Hence, a core principle of American democracy—freedom of expression—is eroded.

My initial reaction to this message was to dispute it. I have seen no hint of self-censoring among my students, and I was inclined to doubt the relevance of the only evidence I heard to support the claim, which was that 80% of college students have reported self-censorship;[36] that, I thought to myself, tells us nothing about K-12 students. But I know that debating these points achieves little and that my experience may belie that of other teachers in other schools. So I stuck to searching for common ground.

Freedom of expression is not only a common American value; it is a widely embraced ideal of education—among those who are and are not "woke." In my school, we worked hard to encourage healthy risk-taking among our students—whether trying a new sport or performing on stage or speaking up without being sure of the "answer." This is an easy point of agreement among educators and parents—that we want children to exercise their voices. If we strip this issue out of the national discourse, separate it from the warring tribes, and approach it with good intent, teachers and parents alike can absolutely agree that we wish for our students to appreciate the power and privilege of freedom of expression and that we aspire for them to exercise this right.

The perils of obedience: Closely related to freedom of expression is a wariness about obedience and conformity. Elana Fishbein, who is Israeli, evoked the Holocaust during her presentation in saying that people fear speaking up about what is happening in schools. "And we know what happens when we're afraid and we don't stand up."[37] I am certainly not one to contest this concern, when, for years, Martin Niemoller's famous quote greeted students at my classroom door: "First they came for the socialists—and I did not speak out because I was not a socialist.... Then they came for the Jews, and I did not speak out—because I am not a Jew. Then they came for me—and there was no one left to speak for me."[38] As a supplement to our Holocaust unit, my colleagues and I would show students footage of Stanley Milgram's famous experiment on obedience in which study participants administered what they believed were ever-higher levels of electrical shock despite hearing the anguished cries of those subjected to the shocks, simply because they were told to.[39] I can get behind a skepticism of blind obedience.

Still, the instinctive response among many educators to Fishbein's concern would almost certainly be affront: *She is comparing diversity programming to the Third Reich?* If we can take a breath and allow the emotional flush of that response to fade, though, we will position ourselves to see the common cause intrinsic to Fishbein's concern—no one wishes for our children to become overly conformist automatons. We can start with that.

Civil discourse: As a logical extension of the concern about conformity and freedom of expression, some parents worry that students' critical thinking skills are dulled by a lack of dialogue across lines of ideological difference. A parent group called New Trier Neighbors, for example, encouraged their school board to adopt a written commitment to "Critical Thinking & Civil Discourse."[40] Any reader who was not put to sleep by the first seven chapters of this book will know that I, too, support this goal, and I see a great irony at play in the impasse between these parent groups and mainstream educators. Often, I speak with friends in the world of education who ask what I've been doing since leaving the classroom. When I say I am at work on a book that contends schools have a role to play in helping to depolarize the country, they almost universally respond with some form of, "Wow. And you think parents are going to allow that?"

The national screaming match between schools and parent groups conceals a fundamental, shared goal. Every educator I know counts critical thinking as a core competency (see Chapter Three). Parents value it too, yet some believe critical thinking is incompatible with an emphasis on diversity, equity, and inclusion (which I am working hard to understand), leading to the assumption that it's one or the other—DEI or critical thinking. In fact, though, we all agree on this point: there is great value in asking kids to think critically, and we strive to provide opportunities for them to do so.

And others: In many other ways, too, I found areas of common ground with the speakers who presented at the Parents Unite conference, despite my fundamental disagreement with their characterization of diversity, equity, and inclusion initiatives as an attack on their children and country. Race is divisive—we agree on that. We agree, too, on transparency—that it is reasonable for parents to know what is going on in their children's schools. We agree, as well, that kids deserve to be their authentic selves. This is the very essence, as I have always understood it, of the push for diversity, equity, and inclusion—to allow each student to be fully seen, heard, and appreciated for the full extent of their identity. That some parents understand DEI work to constitute an attack on that principle must not obscure the fact that we agree on the principle itself. In many other ways, if we are willing to listen to each other, we will find what we have in common.

Dialogue Among Parents Who Disagree

There are people working hard to find commonalities between those who support and those who oppose diversity, equity, and inclusion initiatives in schools. One of them is Lamont Turner. An executive coach, author, and Tennessee parent, Turner was the only Black male in his high school graduating class. He is experienced in gently navigating the line of sensitive racial discussions that lurk mostly beneath the consciousness of his largely white community, and he is supportive of the efforts of a local group called One WillCo to boost diversity, equity, and inclusion efforts in local schools. He is also blessed with patience and empathy, traits that have positioned him to engage in conversation with Robin Steenman, founder of the local chapter of Moms for Liberty, who opposes those efforts.[41]

For many years, Turner sold medical devices, and he draws on his professional experience to describe his approach to dialogue. Racism has left wounds, he says, and truth is the nutrient that will heal those wounds, with conversation serving as the blood flow to deliver that nutrient. In that spirit, when Steenman reached out to him for a conversation, Turner accepted the invitation. Turner had attended a public meeting during which Moms for Liberty shared their viewpoint of critical race theory, a gathering he found to be emotionally charged and laced, as he put it, with "showmanship."[42]

Committed to dialogue, though, Turner began attending smaller Moms for Liberty meetings, which featured a more civil tone than the contentious public gatherings grabbing the headlines. "I saw their humanity," Turner says.[43] He had shared his own humanity, too, sending Steenman a picture of his daughters at play in their living room, and he and Steenman have maintained a steady stream of communication. As this book went into production, Turner intended to hold a symposium at his former high school, to feature a conversation between the founders of One WillCo and Robin Steenman.

Similar conversations will need to happen all over the country. Like Turner, I have plans to bring people to the table. In my case, I have proposed gathering a small group of educators who are committed to DEI initiatives in schools and a small group of parents who oppose that work, to share the stage during an event such as the National Week of Conversation.[44] As was the case with Brookwood's IDEA meetings among faculty, such a dialogue would provide an opportunity for those on either side of the impasse to share their personal stories and engage in deep listening. If such a conversation comes to pass, there will be no debate, only the search for understanding.

What Schools Can Do

Schools that are interested in holding similar conversations with parents might look to the model used by Brookwood's science department in their human sexuality programming. Like race, gender and sexuality are discussion topics fraught with danger, and over the years Brookwood's human sexuality unit has reliably stirred up concern among parents, with the bulk of that angst trained on the science teachers who shoulder the responsibility for teaching the unit. Weary of the challenges that came their way each spring, Brookwood asked human sexuality guru, Deborah Roffman, for help. Her advice: instead of leading with the content, start with a set of shared values.

For years, the science department had begun the human sexuality unit by sending home a lengthy letter laying out the rationale for and the details of the coming curricular programing. It was a content-heavy overture. Under Roffman's tutelage, though, Brookwood began hosting parent meetings that focused not on the content of the unit but on building a sense of community.

One teacher would run a "four corners" exercise in which parents would arrange themselves in the room according to their responses to statements such as "I received most of my teaching on this topic from friends or family." The exercise revealed shared experiences and engendered a feeling of trust. "It was a great conversation starter," says former Department Head Annie Johnson. "Parents discovered so much in common."[45]

The conversation would then turn to values. "Tell me" a teacher would ask the parents. "What are the characteristics you would hope to see embodied in our graduates?" A list would materialize: parents would, year after year, hope for graduates to be kind and compassionate, to be critical thinkers, to be knowledgeable, to be confident. Eventually, the conversation would come around to the main point: that the human sexuality unit upon which teachers were about to embark was a vehicle to help build these traits. Viewed in this light, the curriculum felt less threatening, more understandable. Approaching the start of the unit this way did not dissolve every concern of every parent, but it made the experience smoother for parents, teachers, and students.

These are the conversations schools need to be having with parents: exploration of shared values, to disrupt the "us" versus "them" paradigm that will otherwise hijack every attempt we make to broach worthwhile, contentious topics. And individual teachers can implement the approach. Just as we seek to build a collective responsibility for norms of behavior among our students, so too can we teachers identify a shared pool of goals and aspirations with the parents of our students by asking them to share those goals. In time, those goals will be tested. A parent may wonder why so much class time is devoted to dialogue, or why a Fox News segment appeared during the current-events lesson, or what the reasoning could be to feature a particular novel in the curriculum.

The answers to those questions should always be that they serve as vehicles to deliver children toward one or more of the community's shared goals. In the absence of a pool of shared values or goals, we run the risk of parents situating a teaching strategy or curricular resource within the narrative of polarization that swirls around us: *the Fox News segment is evidence of the teacher's political agenda; the emphasis on dialogue is proof of indoctrination.* In the face of such accusations, we are defenseless, because the threats that people read into those activities disable rational thinking. Every element of our society pushes these interactions toward the intractable impasse of polarization. We must start from a place of shared understanding and build from there.

Conclusion: Leave the Battlefield Behind

On the Moms for Liberty website, a map allows the user to search for local chapters of the organization. Above that map is a single sentence that sums up our troubles: "Find your people."[46] Polarization is not principally about ideas. It's about group membership—about our inclination to seek safety within the group, to rally around the symbols and messaging of our group, and to mistrust the other group.

It is curious that the Moms for Liberty website would draw my attention, and that I would discover that the founder of one of its local chapters is in conversation with Lamont Turner, because it turns out that I have been there, to the site of that dialogue, in Franklin, Tennessee.

Before traveling to Birmingham and watching for the ghost of Bull Connor, before partnering my students with their counterparts in Alabama, I first attempted that project with a school in Franklin, and that school happens to be the one Lamont Turner attended.

Like hundreds of places throughout the South, Franklin is the site of a Civil War battle, and when I visited my partner school, I also toured the local points of interest. As I stood next to a bullet-riddled home there, preserved as a museum, I did something I had never done before: I thought deeply about what it would have been like to live on the Confederate side of the war. "Imagine you are here, in your home, and you look out over that field." A docent, patient and knowledgeable, pointed north. "You have been told that a huge army is coming across that land to kill you and your family." I looked, trying to imagine the dread. "That, for you, is the war." For some white southerners of modest means, the war was not about ideology. It was simply about self-preservation. The war did not become relevant for those people, the docent said, until it arrived on their land. This really got my head spinning. The war was, irrefutably, fought to preserve slavery. But it is *also* true that, for some people, the war was as simple as defending hearth and home.

For many of the fervent opponents of DEI work, this is today's war, as well: the defense of hearth and home. Schools' diversity initiatives have become attached, as perceived by their opponents, to a broader, liberal agenda, which itself is associated with the out-group, characterized by some as a marauding force bent on destruction. It should come as no surprise, then, to behold the energy with which some are attempting to repel that attack. Parents exist, after all, to defend their children.[47]

Eventually, perhaps even by the time this book goes to print, the battle may not be about race. Two years ago, after all, I had never heard of "critical race theory"—and I had led diversity initiatives among my colleagues and spent two decades teaching children about the intersection of race and constitutional law. As quickly as the topic emerged, then, it may give way to gender or some other issue that magnifies our divisiveness. But, even in that case, we are sure to face some sort of impasse, energized by the polarization that cripples us in other areas.

That impasse will consequently prime some parents to stay in a defensive mode that, ironically, hampers our attempts to position their children to eventually navigate a polarized society. Because, for those children to do so, they must have ample opportunities to reach across lines of divide. This will require them to do things like listen deeply to people with whom they may not agree or to vary their media diet. These experiences may feel innocuous to the classroom teacher who plans them, yet they may feel threatening to a parent who perceives them to be markers of an attack. We educators will play a perpetual and unwinnable game in which we lob back the challenges parents serve up to us until we accept that we are all impacted by the polarization that grips the country. Which also means that we run the risk of discarding parents' concerns, as we more broadly are inclined to do with anything that challenges our identities. They will defend against the attack they perceive, while we do the same.

Unless we start from scratch, by engaging parents in conversations that help us build a common starting point. We need to open the lines of communication to discover that we operate with a common motivation—to serve our children. And from there, we must identify common goals, such as helping kids learn to care for others, to appreciate different points of view, to think critically. Only when we have established that common ground will we have a shot at disabling the automatic processes that hamper our collaboration. Only then will we be able to implement the classroom practices that will help prepare our students to meet the needs of society.

So, fundamentally, the bridge-building work that we propose for our children, and that we ask of our faculty, also requires the participation of parents because without parents the enterprise will fail. Ultimately, if we want kids to reach across lines of divide, we adults need to show them how to do so.

Notes

1   Lautzenheiser et al., 2011
2   McAvoy & Hess, 2013, p. 31
3   McAvoy & Hess, 2013, p.32
4   No Left Turn in Education, 2021
5   Parents Defending Education, 2022
6   Anderson & Brugal, 2021
7   New Trier Neighbors, 2021
8   Miller, 2022
9   Miller, 2022
10 Schwartz & Pendharkar, 2022
11 Schwartz & Pendharkar, 2022
12 Schwartz & Pendharkar, 2022
13 Fox News, 2020 "Exposing the left's…"
14 Fox News, 2020 "Trump administration wants to end…"

15   Fox News, 2020 "Trump administration wants to end…"
16   Stelter, 2020
17   Rufo, 2020
18   Exec. Order No. 13950, 2020
19   Exec. Order No. 13958, 2020
20   Stelter, 2020
21   Barr, 2021
22   Jacobson, 2021
23   Moms for Liberty, 2022 "Who We Are"
24   Parents Unite, 2021. See "Starting a Grassroots Movement."
25   Fox News, 2020 "Trump administration wants to end…"
26   Stelter, 2020
27   Fox News, 2021
28   Exec. Order No. 13950, 2020
29   Cineas, 2020
30   Critical Race Training in Education, 2020–2022
31   Parents Unite, 2021. See "Starting a Grassroots Movement."
32   Miller, 2022
33   Anderson & Brugal, 2021
34   Waytz et al., 2014
35   Parents Unite, 2021. See "The Fight for Our Schools: What's at Stake."
36   Parents Unite, 2021. See "Confronting the Crisis in Our Schools & Adopting the Chicago Statement."
37   Parents Unite, 2021. See "Starting a Grassroots Movement."
38   United States Holocaust Memorial Museum, 2012
39   Facing History and Ourselves, 2022
40   New Trier Neighbors "How to pass a high school 'Chicago Statement'"
41   Sheasley, 2022
42   Turner, 2022
43   Turner, 2022
44   America Talks, 2022
45   Johnson, 2022
46   Moms for Liberty, 2022
47   The backlash against DEI work in schools has been supercharged by the dynamic of polarization. However, I do not discount the sincerity or wisdom that animates some people in their opposition to, or questioning of, aspects of this work. To suggest that

all opponents of DEI work are blindly caught in the whirlwind of polarization would be a discredit to those who have undoubtedly come to their views through careful consideration, rather than instinctive opposition. One example would be Ian Rowe, an experienced educator who, as a parent, was troubled by what he viewed as a flawed equity audit administered by his local school district. His concern deepened when so few in his community risked speaking up about the shortcomings of that audit. Rowe's Parents Unite presentation is thoughtful and measured, and it serves as a reminder to educators committed to DEI work that there is reasonable opposition to the way this work is being implemented in some school districts, aside from the tribal panic that animates many of its opponents. Rowe's presentation, called "Participatory School Governance & Leadership, Courage, Agency, and 'Equity,'" can be found by following the bibliographic entry for "Parents Unite, 2021."

9

Conclusion: Finding the Courage to Depolarize

This is a simple book. Americans are profoundly polarized, and the mountain of evidence supporting this conclusion, gathered over many years, compels us to face the fact that this polarization awaits our students. We must prepare them to meet the challenge.

We educators need not shoulder the exclusive responsibility for depolarizing our country, because elements of our disfunction undoubtedly lie beyond the purview of schools. Some writers, like Senator Ben Sasse, trace our polarization to a crisis of isolation and rootlessness. With the decline of community-based institutions such as church and civic groups, people seek membership where they can find it—and they are finding it on either side of the political divide.[1] Some researchers blame our two-party political system for cleaving the country into warring factions,[2] in which case modifications to our electoral system may provide some relief. The problem is complex, and it must be addressed on a number of fronts. Let us not pretend, though, that education is not one of them.

We are school people, and we deal in the currency of knowledge. We educators hold information in high regard, and we are inclined to see reason as a therapeutic for the malady of polarization. Disagreement over the issues can be assuaged, we

DOI: 10.4324/9781003289494-9

hope, by arming people with facts. But it simply is not enough to know things, because our polarization is not only ideological but also affective. Group membership provides solace, and generally speaking, we do not trust, or like, or respect the political "other." The experience of modern life exacerbates our divisions. We surround ourselves with like-minded thinkers in both our physical and digital worlds, and that seclusion breeds ideological extremity—whatever we think, we come to believe even more deeply. For many people—although we would be quick to deny it—politics has worked its way into our identity. *This is what I think* has become *This is who I am.* We are programmed to perceive a threat to our identity as a threat to the self, and we unconsciously discard or discredit information that challenges our deeply held beliefs. We just aren't built to reappraise our views when those views are central to our self-image.

But our divides, formidable though they are, are not as pronounced as we imagine. We overgeneralize and stereotype. We find the most abhorrent example of the "other" and convince ourselves that all members of the opposing tribe are that way. And we assume that those people find us more repellent than is actually the case. We also tend to overestimate our ideological disagreements, and on many issues, it is still possible for a majority of Americans to find common ground. We can see openings here—reasons to be hopeful that, if we put our backs into it, we will position our students to meet the challenge of polarization.

Doing that work with children is not so complicated. Kids need to engage in dialogue across lines of disagreement from an early age, accumulating and reinforcing listening and speaking skills that will position them to participate in increasingly complex and contentious conversations. They need to meet the "other." This will happen within the classroom, although there may also be creative opportunities to partner children for collaborations beyond the walls of their classrooms. Because emotions are central to polarization, finding our way through this mess requires attention to social emotional learning, and media literacy is indispensable. None of that work, frankly, is particularly tricky, nor is it controversial. A wealth of SEL and media literacy programming is available to educators, and generally speaking, we teachers are pretty handy at facilitating conversations; it's what we do for a living.

The Tool Kit Will Not Suffice

Most of us could get even better at enabling those conversations, though, and we all want the "tool kit" to facilitate dialogue. *Life is busy. Cut to the chase and give us the strategies.* Here, though, I encourage a deep, collective breath. The solution to our challenge does not fundamentally lie in a mastery of classroom mechanics—the implementation of a listening sequence, or the modeling of sentence stems, or some particular conversation protocol. Rather, there is an important prerequisite to that work. The "tool kit" will not get us far without a genuine motivation to implement it, and I am not convinced that we educators have yet marshalled that motivation.

In January of 2022, I tuned in to programming organized for the National Day of Dialogue. Michael Gingerich, co-founder of Someone To Tell It To, made a profound statement, which was that dialogue requires people to first believe the other has something important to say. I'm not sure we educators have made that discovery. In my experience, even the most earnest teachers approach dialogue across difference as an exercise in forbearance. We take a deep breath and allow others to have their say. We tolerate, but do not welcome, the opposing viewpoint, and we warily guard against disclosing our own biases.

Anyone who has ever led students through a norm-building exercise will recognize a familiar dynamic to the conversation. We ask kids how we should treat each other, and they generally begin by saying what should *not* happen: we should not be mean, or interrupt, or sneeze on our neighbor's macaroni and cheese. This is where many of us adults find ourselves: thinking about what *not* to do—how not to tip our hand or say something to alienate a student or offend a parent. But this work cannot be merely about guarding against our impulses. *Excellent*, we say to our students, *so we shouldn't sneeze on the mac and cheese, but what* should *we do? How* should *we act? What does it look like to be respectful?* This is where we teachers need to aim ourselves, too—toward practicing the habits that model genuine curiosity about those with whom we disagree, rather than merely avoiding the behaviors that reveal our own biases. The conversational tool kit will only serve us if we actually want to build the bridges—and if we want that for our students.

Can we find that motivation? When the student shows up with a MAGA hat, will a left-leaning teacher draw from a reservoir of curiosity, or will she freeze in the face of what can only feel like a threat to her group? When parents challenge the DEI curriculum, will teachers circle the wagons, or will they marshal authentic curiosity about the roots of that opposition? Will teachers quickly agree to disagree, or will they enter into a partnership to collectively serve the interest of the student? The answers to these questions depend on the work we adults are willing to do with each other, before even reaching for the tool from that kit. My hunch is that motivation will only come from experience. Until teachers sit together and discover the revelation of hearing the story of someone across the political aisle, until they have themselves yearned to know more, they may implement the "tool kit" of conversational bridge-building in a perfunctory way, as a matter of diligence but not delight.

For now, that work is hampered by our ingrained apprehension about messing with anything "political." Politics is a dirty, dirty word in the world of education, and if there is one thing on which most people (but not I) can agree, it is that politics has no place in school. One of the most common critiques among conservative parent groups is that schools have become "politicized." This is like saying schools have become "oxygenated," yet educators reflexively deny the charge and take pains to avoid the perception that their curriculum or teaching methodologies have been tainted by politicization. *Our emphasis on climate change? No, no, that's not political, it's scientific. Oh, that email we sent out? We don't mean to suggest that Black Lives Matter, but rather that black lives matter. Surely you understand the difference: it's a moral issue, not a political one.* This is a futile and counterproductive battle, and waging it runs the risk of forfeiting the learning our students require to face the challenge itself.

We remove that text from the curriculum, we think twice about inviting that speaker, we shy away from that topic of class discussion. We also avoid the work required of us—such as sitting with our colleagues and listening to their stories—because it smacks of violating that unwritten prohibition on "politics." And because we automatically, inexplicably forbid ourselves from engaging in political talk, we deprive our students of lessons that, in a less polarized world, would be obviously within our purview, such as those gleaned from observing the comportment of our country's leader.

As a candidate for office and as president of the United States, Donald Trump behaved in flagrant violation of the expectations that my school—and every school I know—had set for its own community members. And yet—at least in my experience—we stood by silently throughout the Trump era, wringing our hands while the president acted, day in and day out, in ways that would have landed him in deep trouble in our schools. What sense did students make of this complicity? What unspoken lessons did they learn?

We relinquished our chance to teach important lessons about behavior, about standards of communication, about democratic principles during the Trump presidency because we had not done the work to enable that teaching. We had not established a culture of dialogue across difference that would have laid the groundwork to enter into unavoidably contentious conversations among adults—which would have necessarily complemented conversations with our students—about President Trump. We teachers had not engaged in deep listening to understand the personal narratives that inform difference of political opinion among colleagues. We had not joined with parents to co-create goals for our children that would bind us in times of disagreement. In the absence of that work, we had not established the goodwill and understanding across political divides that would have allowed us to agree on the obvious.

In my school, located next door to the country's most politically intolerant county, we did not trust ourselves to wade into any discussion of the president because we couldn't separate Trump's rhetoric from a wider political identity. To comment on an offensive tweet, we worried, might have implied an attack on conservatism more broadly. We allowed ourselves to be manipulated by the tyranny of polarization, tacitly agreeing—because we could see no other way—that to question the president's behavior was to implicitly malign everything associated with it, including the people who supported him. What a terrible loss. We had golden opportunities—many of them—to ask our students why people back Trump *despite*, not *because of* his behavior. We didn't know how to have the conversation, and rather than figure it out, we let it pass us by.

We are compelled to do this work, then, not only because the long-term health of our country requires a fresh generation of more open-minded, less tribal, more inquisitive citizens to guide our progress. We do this not just for a societal payoff somewhere down the road but also because, right now, our teaching is hamstrung without it. The paralysis of polarization increasingly seeps into everything we teach; science, language, current events, history, literature, art—everything—is imbued with some hint of political polarization. We can continue to allow that polarization to grow, squeezing out more and more of the learning opportunities we would otherwise embrace, or we can acknowledge that polarization, lean into its challenges, and reclaim those moments in our day-to-day interactions with our students.

If there is opposition to this work—aside from the difficulty of admitting that the political world is intertwined with the life of the school—it lies in the concern that we are setting up our students to lose sight of a shared moral compass. Many teachers I know are interested *in theory* in exposing children to diverse perspectives, but they wonder how to do so when some points of view are deplorable. Do we really need to provide balance, they wonder, on topics that only have one reasonable perspective? The question, then, becomes: is "balance" the objective?

In the fall of 2021, Texas passed a state law requiring teachers to avoid teaching controversial issues and, in the event of a contentious topic presenting itself organically, to "explore such issues from diverse and contending perspectives without giving deference to any one perspective."[3] One school official suggested to elementary school teachers that sources on the Holocaust be accompanied by books with "opposing views." As one might imagine, this was not well received, and Texas education officials later took pains to clarify that teaching the Holocaust did not require teachers to condone Holocaust denial.[4] Nonetheless, it is this sort of thing that haunts teachers—that every point of view requires a competing viewpoint in the name of neutrality.

"Balance" is helpful. Two news sources of dueling biases are likely to present a more complete picture of an event than a single source would. Digging up more information might lead a student to a more balanced understanding of an issue than a limited serving of facts would provide. But to prepare students to navigate our polarized society does not call for "balance" as the ultimate ideal. Neutrality is not the holy grail. We do not seek to wash our students (or ourselves) clean of their (or our) convictions. Instead, what is required of our students is understanding. We need for them to have the urge, the unappeasable hunger, to understand what drives people with whom they disagree. Let them be wildly, unabashedly unbalanced in their viewpoints when they have arrived at those positions after careful, well-informed consideration. But help them, amid their certitude, also search exhaustively for the reasons that others disagree.

In Celebration of Ambiguity

But then what? How will understanding lead to cooperation? How is the existential environmental threat managed through "understanding" climate denial? How is the crippling national debt eased, the next pandemic moderated, the impasse over any number of intractable disagreements solved simply by appreciating what makes those people across the aisle tick? The answer, alas, is that I do not know, and frankly, I am at peace not knowing.

Many moons ago, I took a graduate class with Eleanor Duckworth, a legend at Harvard's Graduate School of Education. Duckworth pioneered a pedagogical approach, based on the work of Jean Piaget and Barbel Inholder, known as "critical explor-ation," that acknowledges learning to be driven more by the dis-coveries, interests, and questions of the learner than by a fixed script imposed by a teacher.[5] With six years of teaching under my belt at that point, I had mastered the class syllabus. I knew what to teach, how to teach it, and on which date, two weeks hence, it would have been taught. But Professor Duckworth helped me loosen up a little. It was a perspective that I incorporated into the remainder of my teaching career—or my career to this point, at least: there is value in letting the messiness of learning unfold at its own pace and in its own direction.

It is in that spirit that I admit, without even much sheepish-ness, that I just do not know where our collective learning will take us. This journey of depolarization is too novel. I can see the first bend in the road, the part where we collectively reach some authentic understanding of the "others" from whom we currently feel almost hopelessly estranged. But how we get from there to the point of cooperation, to the collaborative solving of society's problems, remains out of view. Still, I have faith that we will see it eventually. The learning—the learning of teachers, of parents, of students—will unfold if we let it, and we will find our way.

Connecting the Dots

In keeping with Professor Duckworth's philosophy, and that of constructivism more broadly, I do know that finding our way must start with our youngest learners. Decades ago, John Dewey, Jean Piaget, and others figured out that children make sense of their learning by constructing it out of cumulative experiences—one lays the groundwork for the next. At present, then, we are mixed up, because instead of starting at the beginning, the bridge-building movement is backing its way into schools.

A number of promising organizations have emerged to address the national crisis of polarization, but they all seem to target those Americans who are either the most polarized or on the verge of becoming so. Braver Angels started as a conversation among a small group of voters in Ohio, quickly expanded, and now, in addition to providing programming for and conversations among adults, also runs debates among college students. Allsides, with its roots in news literacy, launched a pilot program to partner university students for cross-cutting conversations and then adapted the program for high school and then middle school students. The Better Arguments Project, like Braver Angels, first targeted adults before partnering with me to create a curriculum for middle and high school students. It is the case with every bridge-building institution I know that the work began with adults before backing its way into schools (if it has made its way into schools at all).

From my perspective, though, as a veteran of a pre-K-through-eight school, we've got this backwards. In fact, we should be thinking about the work as a habit that begins among the youngest students when they wield their "star" and "heart" sticks at ages four and five, to be reinforced as they make their way toward adulthood. And in order to reinforce that learning, we need to help students connect the dots. It would be easy for kids to lose track of the significance of any single experience that serves the goal of depolarization, because the skill of bridge-building lies outside the purview of school structures that establish and track the scope and sequence of traditional disciplines; there is no Department of Depolarization in our schools to knit together the seemingly disparate learning experiences that, collectively, could help prepare our children for a polarized world. Serious bridge-building work is not confined to a social studies classroom. It will appear across the disciplines, and it relies on social emotional learning and media literacy, which, when done well, are integrated throughout the curriculum.

A forward-thinking school may weave powerful social and emotional learning into its curriculum, and it may feature robust training in media literacy. Furthermore, it could be a place of lively cross-cutting dialogue in which students are wrestling with matters of importance among people who see the world differently. But it may not recognize the mutually reinforcing nature of these learning experiences, because they exist under different organizational umbrellas. And if the school doesn't see the full constellation, there's no way it can connect the dots for children to show them how seemingly unrelated experiences across domain and grade level could work to bolster their ability to build bridges across lines of divide. We must find this clarity and provide the guidance that will help students identify their growth as bridge-builders.

For high school, I attended Friends School of Baltimore, which appealed mostly because, unlike the school I had earlier attended, it had girls. It also had meeting for worship, a gathering that, in its silence, I initially found unbearably funny. The experience was not entirely wasted on me though, as maturity brought a greater appreciation for the clarity that comes from quietude. For some educators, answering the challenge of polarization will come as a spiritual calling, perhaps akin to the experience of sitting quietly in a meetinghouse and listening for the voice of God that, some believe, exists in all of us. For others, it might be a sense of patriotism that moves us to action—the earnest belief that, for this country to keep running, we need to do this work with kids. Or it might just be a matter of professionalism—the dutiful recognition that, among other 21st century skills, children will need to arm themselves with bridge-building skills to thrive.

Whatever the case, the foundation of a responsible citizenry that engages across lines of disagreement lies unavoidably in the domain of education. It bears repeating: the world needs what our children can do, if only we can find the courage to help them do it.

Notes

1   Sasse, 2018
2   Drutman, 2020
3   Prose, 2021
4   Hixenbaugh & Hylton, 2021
5   Duckworth, 2001

Appendix: Consolidated List of Resources

A number of resources, scattered across the book, may interest educators. For convenience, they are consolidated here.

Connecting Students Across Classrooms

Confederate Flag Project
For those interested in the cross-country collaboration described in Chapter Four, the blogs from the three school years beginning with 2016–2017 remain accessible for now:
https://brookwoodschool.net/blogs/masondixon1617/
https://brookwoodschool.net/blogs/masondixon1718/
https://brookwoodschool.net/blogs/masondixon1819/

AllSides for Schools (https://allsidesforschools.org/mismatch/)
Has a number of resources to boost news literacy and encourage dialogue among middle and high school students. Their Mismatch program "connects students across distance and divides to engage in respectful, face-to-face conversation."

American Pals (www.americanpals.org/)
A pen pal program for students—"bridging divides and connecting America's classrooms, one letter at a time."

American Exchange Project (https://americanexchangeproject.org/)
A free domestic exchange program that allows high school students to spend a summer living in a different part of the country.

National Constitution Center (https://constitutioncenter.org/ interactive-constitution/online-civic-learning-opportunities)
Offers programs suitable for elementary through high school students (and beyond). Their peer-to-peer scholar exchanges use the Constitution to "promote deeper understanding and enhance opportunities for civil discourse and discussion."

Classroom Norm-Setting and Dialogue

Facing History and Ourselves (www.facinghistory.org/resou rce-library/teaching-strategies/contracting)
Their "contracting" teaching strategy provides guidance on establishing norms of behavior in the classroom.

Learning for Justice (www.learningforjustice.org/sites/default/ files/2021-11/LFJ-2111-Lets-Talk-November-2021-11172021.pdf)
Let's Talk is a lengthy, detailed guide, full of practical, concrete suggestions to lead critical conversations across all grade ranges.

The Greater Good Science Center's *Bridging Differences Playbook* (https://greatergood.berkeley.edu/ima ges/uploads/Bridging_Differences_Playbook-Final.pdf)
Dozens of lessons to help students reach across ideological divides. Try pages 44–50: "Listen with Compassion" and "Put People Before Politics."

The Better Arguments Project (https://betterarguments.org/ resources-tabs/#education)
Resources for middle and high school students include a six-session curriculum to facilitate conversations across lines of difference.

OpenMind (https://openmindplatform.org/content/)
OpenMind explores the science that explains our divisions and provides suggestions to reach across lines of divide. An eight-session curriculum helps high school students do so.

Teaching Made Practical (https://teachingmadepractical.com/facilitating-small-group-discussion/)
This website has some good suggestions for structuring small-group conversations in the upper-elementary classroom.

Cult of Pedagogy (www.cultofpedagogy.com/speaking-listening-techniques/)
Another website with ideas for structuring class discussions.

Recent Films to Inspire Bridge-Building Work

Dialogue Lab: America (https://ideosinstitute.org/dla)
Presents a promising model of face-to-face, cross-cutting political discussion.

Reunited States (https://reunitedstates.tv/)
A powerful documentary that exposes our national rift and provides hope for mending it.

For the Common Good (https://vimeo.com/tnpideafilms/review/383616248/665271ed21)
A short film documenting a public conflict between Simon Greer and Fox News host Glenn Beck and their one-on-one conversation in search of understanding and closure in its wake.

SEL and Media Literacy

CASEL (https://casel.org/)
The go-to authority on social emotional learning. Their _3 Signature Practices Playbook_ is an excellent resource, as are many other resources available through CASEL.

Center for Healthy Minds (https://centerhealthyminds.org/)
An initiative of the University of Wisconsin-Madison. Their many resources include the Mindfulness-Based Kindness Curriculum for Preschoolers.

Center for Media Literacy (www.medialit.org/global-ramp-media-literacy)
A hub of research and resources in the field of media literacy.

National Association for Media Literacy Education (https://namle.net/)
Searching for media literacy resources? NAMLE is a good place to start.

Common Sense Media (www.commonsense.org/education/digital-citizenship)
Common Sense is a highly regarded organization. See the Digital Life Resource Center for lessons to use in K-12 classrooms.

The Social Dilemma (www.thesocialdilemma.com/)
An important documentary, appropriate for middle and high school students.

Balancing the News Diet

Read Across the Aisle (www.readacrosstheaisle.com/)
An app that gathers news from across the political spectrum and monitors the user's choice of media outlets.

AllSides (www.allsides.com/unbiased-balanced-news)
A good site to visit when looking for a range of news from left, right, and center.

Ground News (https://ground.news/)
Provides varied news coverage, helps the user monitor the bias of news intake, and has an interesting feature called "Blindspot" that flags stories being covered exclusively or heavily by media from just one side of the political spectrum.

The Flip Side (www.theflipside.io/)
Delivers news each day on a single story from both sides of the political spectrum.

Tangle (www.readtangle.com/)
A newsletter that aggregates reporting from both sides of the aisle.

Adults Practicing Dialogue Across Divides

Braver Angels (https://braverangels.org/)
A rapidly growing organization that produces compelling programming—podcasts, webinars, debates, etc.—intended to depolarize America.

Living Room Conversations (https://livingroomconversations.org/)
Connects people across the country for guided conversations. "Healing divides starts with conversation."

Greater Good Science Center Bridging Differences Initiative (https://ggsc.berkeley.edu/what_we_do/major_initiatives/bridging_differences)
An excellent source of accessible articles that distill the research on polarization.

Pew Research Center (www.pewresearch.org/politics/2014/06/12/political-polarization-in-the-american-public/)
A highly regarded think tank, producers of indispensable polling information and research on political polarization.

Citizen Connect (https://citizenconnect.us/)
A directory of bridge-building events and organizations.

Parent Rights

Parents Unite (www.parentsunite.org/conference-videos)

The videos from the 2021 Parents Unite conference provide an excellent resource for educators trying to understand what animates the opposition to diversity initiatives in schools. As this book went into production, a conference was also scheduled for the fall of 2022.

Works Cited

Abramowitz, A. I., & Saunders, K. L. (2008). Is polarization a myth? *The Journal of Politics*, *70*(2), 542–555.

Ahler, D., & Sood, G. (2018). The parties in our heads: Misperceptions about party composition and their consequences. *The Journal of Politics*, *80*(3), 964–981.

Alford, J. R., Funk, C. L., & Hibbing, J. R. (2005). Are political orientations genetically transmitted? *American Political Science Review*, *99*(2), 153–167.

AllSides. (n.d.). *News*. Retrieved from AllSides: www.allsides.com/unbia sed-balanced-news

AllSides for Schools. (2021). *Preparing students for thoughtful participation in democracy—and in life*. Retrieved from AllSides for Schools: https://allsidesforschools.org/

America Talks. (2022). *National Week of Conversation 2022*. Retrieved from America Talks: https://americatalks.us/national-week-of-conversation/

American Association of Colleges and Universities (2022). *International Journal of ePortfolio*. Retrieved from International Journal of ePortfolio: www.theijep.com/

American Exchange Project. (2020). Retrieved from American Exchange Project: https://americanexchangeproject.org/media/

American Pals. (n.d.). Retrieved from American Pals: www.americanp als.org/

Anderson, Z., & Brugal, S. (2021, December 29). Moms for liberty: An education army builds. *USA Today*.

Associated Press. (2021, November 12). *New York man arrested after death threat to GOP congressman*. Retrieved from AP: https://apnews.com/article/congress-peter-king-new-york-arrests-926263b51 b1308020a4b8b7f5bc11a78

Baddour, D. (2015, May 14). Almost half of U.S. voters are concerned with Jade Helm—but why? Retrieved from San Francisco

Chronicle:www.sfchronicle.com/news/houston-texas/texas/article/Jade-Helm-Alex-Jones-Greg-Abbott-Department-of-6263358.php

Bail, C., Argyle, L., Brown, T., Bumpus, J., Chen, H., Hunzaker, M., ... Volfovsky, A. (2018). Exposure to opposing views on social media can increase political polarization. *Proceedings of the National Academy of Sciences*, *115*(37), 9216–9221.

Banke, R. (2020). Facilitating politically sensitive discussions. Retrieved from Independent Teacher: www.nais.org/magazine/independent-teacher/spring-2020/facilitating-politically-sensitive-discussions/

Barber, M., & Pope, J. (2019). Does party trump ideology? Disentangling party and ideology in America. *American Political Science Review*, *113*(1), 38–54.

Baron, A. S., Carey, S., & Dunham, Y. (2011). Consequences of "minimal" group affiliations in children. *Child Development*, *82*(3), 793–811.

Barr, J. (2021, October 6). Critical race theory was the hot topic on Fox News this summer. Not so much anymore. Retrieved from Washington Post: www.washingtonpost.com/media/2021/10/06/fox-news-critical-race-theory/

Beck, J. (2017, March 3). This article won't change your mind. Retrieved from The Atlantic: www.theatlantic.com/science/archive/2017/03/this-article-wont-change-your-mind/519093/

Berardino, M. (2012, November 9). Mike Tyson explains one of his most famous quotes. Retrieved from South Florida Sun Sentinel: www.sun-sentinel.com/sports/fl-xpm-2012-11-09-sfl-mike-tyson-explains-one-of-his-most-famous-quotes-20121109-story.html

Bishop, B. (2008). *The big sort: Why the clustering of like-minded America is tearing us apart*. Boston: Houghton Mifflin.

Brackett, M. (2019). *Permission to feel: Unlocking the power of emotions to help our kids, ourselves, and our society thrive*. New York: Celadon Books.

Brady, W., Willis, J., Burkart, D., Jost, J., & Van Bevel, J. (2019). An ideological asymmetry in the diffusion of moralized content on social media among political leaders. *Journal of Experimental Psychology*, *148*(10), 1802–1813.

Braver Angels. (2020). *We bring reds, blues, and others together to talk, listen, and understand.* Retrieved from Braver Angels: https://brave rangels.org/what-we-do/

Bremmer, I. (2020, June 12). The best global responses to the COVID-19 pandemic, 1 year later. Retrieved from Time: https://time.com/5851633/best-global-responses-covid-19/

Brookwood School. (2021). *Our approach.* Retrieved from Brookwood School: https://brookwood.edu/about/our-approach/

Carnegie Corporation of New York, CIRCLE. (2003). *The civic mission of schools.* New York: Carnegie Corporation of New York.

Carsey, T. M., & Layman, G. C. (2006). Changing sides or changing minds? Party identification and policy preferences in the American electorate. *American Journal of Political Science, 50*(2), 464–477.

CASEL. (2019). *SEL 3 signature practices playbook.* Retrieved from CASEL: https://schoolguide.casel.org/resource/three-signature-sel-practices-for-the-classroom/

CASEL. (2022). *Advancing social and emotional learning.* Retrieved from CASEL: https://casel.org/

CASEL. (2022). *SEL in the classroom.* Retrieved from CASEL: https://casel.org/systemic-implementation/sel-in-the-classroom/

CASEL. (2022). *What is the CASEL framework?* Retrieved from CASEL: https://casel.org/fundamentals-of-sel/what-is-the-casel-framew ork/#self-management

Chang, R., Varley, K., Tam, F., Lung, N., & Munoz, M. (2022, January 27). *The best and worst places to be as we learn to live with Covid.* Retrieved from Bloomberg: www.bloomberg.com/graphics/covid-resilie nce-ranking/

Cineas, F. (2020, September 24). *Critical race theory, and Trump's war on it, explained.* Retrieved from Vox: www.vox.com/2020/9/24/21451 220/critical-race-theory-diversity-training-trump

Civic Health Project. (n.d.). Retrieved from Civic Health Project: www.civ ichealthproject.org/

Cohen, G. L. (2003). Party over policy: The dominating impact of group influence on political beliefs. *Journal of Personality and Social Psychology, 85*(5), 808–822.

Collins, C. (2021). Reimagining digital literacy education to save ourselves. Retrieved from Learning for Justice: www.learningforjustice. org/magazine/fall-2021/reimagining-digital-literacy-education-to-save-ourselves

Common Sense Media. (n.d.). *Digital citizenship curriculum*. Retrieved from Common Sense Education: www.commonsense.org/educat ion/digital-citizenship/curriculum?grades=6%2C7%2C8

Common Sense Media. (n.d.). *SEL in digital life resource center*. Retrieved from Common Sense Education: www.commonsense.org/educat ion/SEL

Critical Race Training in Education. (2020–2022). *About this website*. Retrieved from Critical Race Training in Education: https://criticalr ace.org/critical-race-theory-today/

Cuncic, A. (2021, June 22). *Amygdala hijack and the fight or flight response*. Retrieved from Verywell Mind: www.verywellmind.com/what-happens-during-an-amygdala-hijack-4165944

De-Wit, L., van der Linden, S., & Brick, C. (2019, July 2). What are the solutions to political polarization? Retrieved from Greater Good Magazine: https://greatergood.berkeley.edu/article/item/what_are_ the_solutions_to_political_polarization

Dimock, M., & Wike, R. (2020, November 13). *America is exceptional in the nature of its political divide*. Retrieved from Pew Research Center: www.pewresearch.org/fact-tank/2020/11/13/america-is-exceptional-in-the-nature-of-its-political-divide/

Dorison, C. A., Minson, J. A., & Rogers, T. (2019). Selective exposure partly relies on faulty affective forecasts. *Cognition*, *188*, 98–107.

Druckman, J., Gubitz, S., Levendusky, M., & Lloyd, A. (2019). How incivility on partisan media (de)polarizes the electorate. *The Journal of Politics*, *81*(1), 291–295.

Druckman, J., Klar, S., Krupnikov, Y., Levendusky, M., & Ryan, J. B. (2022). (Mis-)estimating affective polarization. *The Journal of Politics*, *84*(2), 1106–1117.

Drutman, L. (2020, January 7). America is now the divided republic the framers feared. Retrieved from The Atlantic: www.theatlantic.com/ ideas/archive/2020/01/two-party-system-broke-constitution/ 604213/

Duckworth, E. (2001). *"Tell Me More:" Listening to Learners Explain*. New York: Teachers College Press.

Dunn, A. (2020, August 24). *Trump's approval ratings so far are unusually stable—and deeply partisan*. Retrieved from Pew Research Center: www.pewresearch.org/fact-tank/2020/08/24/trumps-approval-ratings-so-far-are-unusually-stable-and-deeply-partisan/

Edmonson, C. (2021, November 10). House Republicans who backed infrastructure bill face vicious backlash. Retrieved from New York Times: www.nytimes.com/2021/11/10/us/politics/republicans-backlash-infrastructure-bill.html

Exec. Order No. 13950, 3 C.F.R. 60683–60689 (2020, September 22). Retrieved from https://trumpwhitehouse.archives.gov/president ial-actions/executive-order-combating-race-sex-stereotyping/

Exec. Order No. 13958, 3 C.F.R. 70951–70954 (2020, November 2). Retrieved from https://trumpwhitehouse.archives.gov/president ial-actions/executive-order-establishing-presidents-advisory-1776-commission/

Facing History and Ourselves. (2022). *Contracting*. Retrieved from Facing History and Ourselves: www.facinghistory.org/resource-library/teaching-strategies/contracting

Facing History and Ourselves. (2022). *Obedience: The Milgram Experiment*. Retrieved from Facing History and Ourselves: www.facinghistory.org/resource-library/video/obedience-milgram-experiment

Finkel, E. J., Bail, C. A., Cikara, M., Ditto, P. H., Iyengar, S., Klar, S., … Druckman, J. (2020). Political sectarianism in America. *Science*, *370*(6516), 533–536.

Fishkin, J., Siu, A., Diamond, L., & Bradburn, N. (2021). Is deliberation an antidote to extreme partisan polarization? Reflections on "America in One Room." *American Political Science Review*, *115*(4), 1464–1481.

For the Common Good. (n.d.). Retrieved from For the Common Good: https://vimeo.com/tnpideafilms/review/383616248/665 271ed21

Fox News. (2020, July 17). *Exposing the left's radical "critical race theory."* Retrieved from Fox News: https://video.foxnews.com/v/617230 2251001#sp=show-clips

Fox News. (2020, September 2). *Trump administration wants to end race-based trainings for federal employees, official claims*. Retrieved from Fox News: www.foxnews.com/politics/trump-admin-trainings-racism

Fox News. (2021, April 18). Woke culture "infecting schools," turning education into indoctrination: "Woke Inc." author. Retrieved from Fox News: https://video.foxnews.com/v/6249327432001#sp=show-clips

Freire, P. (1970). *Pedagogy of the oppressed*. New York: Herder and Herder.

Galston, W. (2010, November 4). *President Barack Obama's first two years: Policy accomplishments, political difficulties*. Retrieved from Brookings: www.brookings.edu/research/president-barack-obamas-first-two-years-policy-accomplishments-political-difficulties/

Gehlbach, H. (2017). Learning to walk in another's shoes. *Phi Delta Kappan, 98*(6), 8–12.

Gift, K., & Gift, T. (2015). Does politics influence hiring? Evidence from a randomized experiment. *Political Behavior, 37*(3), 653–675.

Goldberg, J. (2013, April 12). *Why is the press ignoring the Kermit Gosnell story?* Retrieved from Bloomberg: www.bloomberg.com/opinion/articles/2013-04-12/why-is-the-press-ignoring-the-kermit-gosnell-story-

Goldberg, J. (2020, November 16). Why Obama fears for our democracy. Retrieved from The Atlantic: www.theatlantic.com/ideas/archive/2020/11/why-obama-fears-for-our-democracy/617087/

Goldman, A. (2016, December 7). The Comet Ping Pong gunman answers our reporter's questions. Retrieved from New York Times: www.nytimes.com/2016/12/07/us/edgar-welch-comet-pizza-fake-news.html

Goleman, D. (1995). *Emotional intelligence*. New York: Bantam Books.

Gonch, W. (2016). *A crisis in civic education*. American Council of Trustees and Alumni.

Gonzalez, J. (2015, October 15). *The big list of class discussion strategies*. Retrieved from Cult of Pedagogy: www.cultofpedagogy.com/speaking-listening-techniques/

Goodreads. (n.d.). *William F. Buckley Jr.* Retrieved from Goodreads: www.goodreads.com/quotes/674-liberals-claim-to-want-to-give-a-hearing-to-other

Greater Good Science Center. (n.d.). *Bridging differences playbook*. Retrieved from Greater Good Science Center: https://greatergood.berkeley.edu/images/uploads/Bridging_Differences_Playbook-Final.pdf

Greer, S. (2021, January 19). Can deep listening heal our divisions? Retrieved from Greater Good Magazine: https://greatergood.berkeley.edu/article/item/can_deep_listening_heal_our_divisions

Ground News. (n.d.). Retrieved from Ground News: https://ground.news/

Haidt, J. (2012). *The righteous mind*. New York: Pantheon Books.

Handler, J. S., & Tuite, Jr., M. L. (2009). *Retouching history: The modern falsification of a Civil War photograph*. Retrieved from Jerome Handler: https://jeromehandler.org/wp-content/uploads/Ret ouching-History-05.pdf

Hart, W., Albarracín, D., Eagly, A. H., Brechan, I., Lindberg, M. J., & Merrill, L. (2009). Feeling validated versus being correct: A meta-analysis of selective exposure to information. *Psychological Bulletin, 135*(4), 555–588.

Hawkins, S., & Raghuram, T. (2020). *American fabric: Identity and belonging*. More in Common. Retrieved from More in Common: www.morei ncommon.com/media/s5jhgpx5/moreincommon_americanfabri creport.pdf

Headlee, C. (2015, April). *10 ways to have a better conversation* [Video]. TED Conferences. Retrieved from TED: www.ted.com/talks/celeste_ headlee_10_ways_to_have_a_better_conversation?language=en

Heritage Not Hate Productions. (2007, November 19). *A tribute to our Black Confederate heroes* [Video]. Retrieved from YouTube: www. youtube.com/watch?v=_GVIAypsnh8

Hess, D. E., & McAvoy, P. (2015). *The political classroom*. New York and London: Routledge.

Hixenbaugh, M., & Hylton, A. (2021, October 14). *Southlake school leader tells teachers to balance Holocaust books with "opposing" views*. Retrieved from NBC News: www.nbcnews.com/news/us-news/ southlake-texas-holocaust-books-schools-rcna2965

Hobbs, R. (2017). Teaching and learning in a post-truth world. *Educational Leadership, 75*(3), 26–31.

Hochschild, A. R. (2016). *Strangers in their own land*. New York: The New Press.

Huber, G., & Malhotra, N. (2017). Political homophily in social relationships: Evidence from online dating behavior. *The Journal of Politics, 79*(1), 269–283.

I Side With. (n.d.). *2022 Political Quiz*. Retrieved from I Side With: www. isidewith.com/political-quiz

Intergovernmental Panel on Climate Change. (n.d.). *AR6 synthesis report: Climate change 2022*. Retrieved from Intergovernmental Panel on Climate Change: www.ipcc.ch/report/sixth-assessment-rep ort-cycle/

Israel, T. (2020, October 12). *How to listen—really listen—to someone you don't agree with*. Retrieved from IDEAS.TED.COM: https://ideas.ted.com/how-to-listen-really-listen-to-some one-you-dont-agree-with/

Iyengar, S., & Hahn, K. (2009). Red media, blue media: Evidence of ideological selectivity in media use. *Journal of Communication, 59*(1),19–39.

Iyengar, S., & Westwood, S. (2015). Fear and loathing across party lines: New evidence on group polarization. *American Journal of Political Science, 59*(3), 690–707.

Iyengar, S., Lelkes, Y., Levendusky, M., Malhotra, N., & Westwood, S. J. (2019). The origins and consequences of affective polarization in the United States. *Annual Review of Political Science, 22*, 129–146.

Jacobs, T. (2018, March 15). The biology of the modern political divide. Retrieved from Greater Good Magazine: https://greatergood.berke ley.edu/article/item/the_biology_of_the_modern_political_ divide

Jacobson, W. A. (2021, December 12). *This is why we fight—2021 Legal Insurrection year-end fundraiser*. Retrieved from Legal Insurrection: https://legalinsurrection.com/2021/12/this-is-why-we-fight-2021-legal-insurrection-year-end-fundraiser/

Jilani, Z. (2019, October 7). How to get some emotional distance in an argument. Retrieved from Greater Good Magazine: https://grea tergood.berkeley.edu/article/item/how_to_get_some_emotio nal_distance_in_an_argument

Johnson, A. (2022, February 18). Personal interview. (K. Lenci, Interviewer).

Journell, W. (2016). Making a case for teacher political disclosure. *Journal of Curriculum Theorizing, 31*(1), 100–111.

Kahan, D. (2015). Climate-science communication and the measure-ment problem. *Advances in Political Psychology, 36*(S1), 1–43.

Kahne, J., & Bowyer, B. (2017). Educating for democracy in a partisan age: Confronting the challenges of motivated reasoning and mis-information. *American Educational Research Journal, 54*(1), 3–34.

Kamarck, E. (2019, September 23). *The challenging politics of climate change*. Retrieved from Brookings: www.brookings.edu/research/ the-challenging-politics-of-climate-change/

Kaplan, J. T., Gimbel, S. I., & Harris, S. (2016). Neural correlates of maintaining one's political beliefs in the face of counterevidence. *Scientific Reports*, *6*, Article 39589.

Klein, E. (2020). *Why we're polarized.* New York: Avid Reader Press.

Kubin, E., Puryear, C., Schein, C., & Gray, K. (2021). Personal experiences bridge moral and political divides better than facts. *Proceedings of the National Academy of Sciences*, *118*(6), 1–9.

Kuh, G. (2008). *High-impact educational practices: What they are, who has access to them, and why they matter.* Washington, DC: Association of American Colleges and Universities.

Langhorne, T. (2018, October 14). *Congress doesn't live here anymore: Secrets of the Hill.* Retrieved from Courier & Press: www.courierpress.com/story/news/2018/10/14/congress-doesnt-live-here-anymore-secrets-hill/1265733002/

Lautzenheiser, D. K., Kelly, A. P., & Miller, C. (2011, June). *AEI program on American citizenship.* Retrieved from: https://files.eric.ed.gov/fulltext/ED521777.pdf

Learning for Justice. (n.d.). *Let's talk: Facilitating critical conversations with students.* Retrieved from Learning for Justice: www.learningforjustice.org/sites/default/files/2021-11/LFJ-2111-Lets-Talk-November-2021-11172021.pdf

Lees, J., & Cikara, M. (2020). Inaccurate group meta-perceptions drive negative out-group attributions in competitive contexts. *Nature Human Behaviour*, *4*(3), 279–286.

Levendusky, M. S. (2018). Americans, not partisans: Can priming American national identity reduce affective polarization? *The Journal of Politics*, *80*(1), 59–70.

Levendusky, M. S., Druckman, J. N., & McLain, A. (2016). How group discussions create strong attitudes and strong partisans. *Research and Politics.* https://doi.org/10.1177/2053168016645137

Lindsay, T. (2020, February 21). Will U.S. education remedy a half-century of neglecting civics education? Retrieved from Forbes: www.forbes.com/sites/tomlindsay/2020/02/21/will-us-education-remedy-a-half-century-of-neglecting-civics-education/?sh=46b646d85fb9

Listen First Project. (2021). Retrieved from Listen First Project: www.listenfirstproject.org/

Living Room Conversations. (2022). Retrieved from Living Room Conversations: https://livingroomconversations.org/

Marks, J., Copland, E., Loh, E., Sunstein, C., & Sharot, T. (2019). Epistemic spillovers: Learning others' political views reduces the ability to assess and use their expertise in nonpolitical domains. *Cognition: International Journal of Cognitive Science, 188*, 74–84.

Mason, L. (2018). *Uncivil agreement: How politics became our identity.* Chicago: University of Chicago Press.

McAvoy, P., & Hess, D. (2013). Classroom deliberation in an era of political polarization. *Curriculum Inquiry, 43*(1),14–47.

McClure, M. (2017, March). *Tackling the American civics education crisis.* Retrieved from National Conference of State Legislators: www.ncsl. org/legislators-staff/legislators/legislators-back-to-school/tackl ing-the-american-civics-education-crisis.aspx

McCormick in Middle (n.d.). *Facilitating small group discussion in the upper elementary classroom.* Retrieved from Teaching Made Practical: https://teachingmadepractical.com/facilitating-small-group-discussion/

Merrefield, C. (2019, December 4). *Massive collection of C-SPAN footage shows Congress members literally cross the aisle less than they used to.* Retrieved from Journalist's Resource: https://journalistsresource. org/politics-and-government/partisan-voting-crossing-the-aisle-linked/

Miller, R. W. (2022, February 1). Virginia's tip line worries educators. *USA Today.*

Minson, J. (2021, March 31). Personal interview. (K. Lenci, Interviewer)

Minson, J., Chen, F., & Tinsley, C. (2020). Why won't you listen to ME? Measuring receptiveness to opposing views. *Management Science, 66*(7), 3069–3094.

Moms for Liberty. (2022). Retrieved from Moms for Liberty: www.mom sforliberty.org/

Moms for Liberty. (2022). *Who we are.* Retrieved from Moms for Liberty: www.momsforliberty.org/about/

Moore-Berg, S. L., Ankori-Karlinsky, L.-O., Hameiri, B., & Bruneau, E. (2020). Exaggerated meta-perceptions predict intergroup hostility between American political partisans. *Proceedings of the National Academy of Sciences, 117*(26), 14864–14872.

Mordecai, M., & Connaughton, A. (2020, October 2020). *Public opinion about coronavirus is more politically divided in U.S. than in other advanced economies*. Retrieved from Pew Research Center: www.pewresearch.org/fact-tank/2020/10/28/public-opinion-about-coronavirus-is-more-politically-divided-in-u-s-than-in-other-advanced-economies/

More in Common. (2019). *The Perception Gap*. Retrieved from More in Common: https://perceptiongap.us/

Mutz, D. (2006). *Hearing the other Side: Deliberative versus participatory democracy*. Cambridge: Cambridge University Press.

National Association for Media Literacy Education (2001). *What is media literacy?* Retrieved from Center for Media Literacy: www.medialit.org/reading-room/what-media-literacy-namles-short-answer-and-longer-thought

National Association for Media Literacy Education. (2021). *The media monsters: A media literacy lesson plan for grade 3–5 educators*. Retrieved from NAMLE: https://namle.net/wp-content/uploads/2021/11/Monsters-Lesson-Plan-1.pdf

National Constitution Center. (2022). *Live online learning*. Retrieved from National Constitution Center: https://constitutioncenter.org/interactive-constitution/online-civic-learning-opportunities

National Council for the Social Studies. (2013). *Revitalizing civic learning in our schools*. Retrieved from National Council for the Social Studies: www.socialstudies.org/position-statements/revitalizing-civic-learning-our-schools

New Trier Neighbors. (n.d.). *How to pass a high school "Chicago Statement."* Retrieved from New Trier Neighbors: www.newtrierneighbors.org/how-to-pass-a-chicago-statement/

New Trier Neighbors. (2021). *About us*. Retrieved from New Trier Neighbors: www.newtrierneighbors.org/about/

Nickerson, C. (2021, November 5). *Allport's intergroup contact hypothesis: Its history and influence*. Retrieved from Simply Psychology: www.simplypsychology.org/contact-hypothesis.html

No Left Turn in Education. (2021). *Mission, Goals & Objectives*. Retrieved from No Left Turn in Education: www.nolefturn.us/mission-goals-objectives/

Nold, C. [@ChristieNold]. (2021, January 6). *Each person knocking down those doors once sat in a classroom* [Tweet]. Retrieved from Twitter: https://twitter.com/ChristieNold/status/134690829225 4216199

Nuclear Threat Initiative. (2019). *Global Health Security Index.* Retrieved from GHS Index: www.ghsindex.org/

Nyhan, B. (2020). Facts and myths about misperceptions. *Journal of Economic Perspectives, 34*(3), 220–236.

O'Connor, C., & Lawson, A. (Hosts). (2021, April 20). High conflict: Why we get trapped and how we get out: Amanda Ripley with Ciaran O'Connor & April Lawson [video podcast episode]. In *The Braver Angels Podcast.* Retrieved from Braver Angels: https://braverang els.org/high-conflict-why-we-get-trapped-and-how-we-get-out-amanda-ripley-with-ciaran-oconnor-april-lawson/

OpenMind. (n.d.). *OpenMind Library.* Retrieved from OpenMind: https:// openmindplatform.org/library/

OpenMind. (n.d.). *OpenMind's virtual learning experience.* Retrieved from OpenMind: https://openmindplatform.org/academic/

Parents Defending Education. (2022). *Empower. Expose. Engage.* Retrieved from Parents Defending Education: https://defendinged.org/

Parents Unite. (2021, October 1–2). *Conference videos.* Retrieved from Parents Unite: www.parentsunite.org/conference-videos

PBS Newshour. (2020, August 17). *Take the Political Party Quiz to find out where you fit!* Retrieved from PBS Newshour: www.pbs.org/newshour/extra/2020/08/take-the-politi cal-party-quiz-to-find-out-where-you-fit/

Pew Research Center. (2016, October 4). *Public knowledge about science has a limited tie to people's beliefs about climate change and climate scientists.* Retrieved from Pew Research Center: www.pewresearch. org/science/2016/10/04/public-knowledge-about-science-has-a-limited-tie-to-peoples-beliefs-about-climate-change-and-clim ate-scientists/

Pew Research Center. (2016, October 4). *The politics of climate.* Retrieved from Pew Research Center: www.pewresearch.org/science/2016/ 10/04/the-politics-of-climate/

Pew Research Center. (2017, October 5). *Global warming and environ-mental regulation, personal environmentalism.* Retrieved from Pew

Research Center: www.pewresearch.org/politics/2017/10/05/7-global-warming-and-environmental-regulation-personal-environmentalism/

Pew Research Center. (2017, October 5). *Partisan animosity, personal politics, views of Trump*. Retrieved from Pew Research Center: www.pewresearch.org/politics/2017/10/05/8-partisan-animosity-personal-politics-views-of-trump/

Pew Research Center. (2017, October 5). *The partisan divide on political values grows even wider*. Retrieved from Pew Research Center: www.pewresearch.org/politics/2017/10/05/the-partisan-divide-on-political-values-grows-even-wider/

Pew Research Center. (2019, December 17). *In a politically polarized era, sharp divides in both partisan coalitions*. Retrieved from Pew Research Center: www.pewresearch.org/politics/2019/12/17/in-a-politically-polarized-era-sharp-divides-in-both-partisan-coalitions/

Pew Research Center. (2021, November 9). *Where do you fit in the political typology?* Retrieved from Pew Research Center: www.pewresearch.org/politics/quiz/political-typology/

Pickett, J., & Lawes, B. (Directors). (2022). *Dialogue lab: America* [Film]. Ideos Institute.

Pierce, L., Rogers, T., & Snyder, J. (2015). Losing hurts: The happiness impact of partisan electoral loss. *Journal of Experimental Political Science, 3*(1), 44–59.

Powers, K. (2013, April 11). Philadelphia abortion clinic horror: Column. Retrieved from USA Today: www.usatoday.com/story/opinion/2013/04/10/philadelphia-abortion-clinic-horror-column/2072577/

Prose, F. (2021, October 19). Texas schools are being told to teach "opposing views" of the Holocaust. Why? Retrieved from The Guardian: www.theguardian.com/commentisfree/2021/oct/19/texas-holocaust-curriculum-schools-hb-3979

Read Across The Aisle (n.d.). *Read Across The Aisle: A Fitbit for your filter bubble*. Retrieved from Read Across The Aisle: www.readacrosstheaisle.com/

Read the document. (2021, February 15). Retrieved from New York Times: www.nytimes.com/interactive/2021/02/15/us/kinzinger-family-letter.html

Rekhi, B. (Director). (2021). *The Reunited States* [Film].

Ripley, A., Tenjarla, R., & He, A. (2019, March 4). The geography of partisan prejudice. *The Atlantic.*

Robb, A. (2017, November 16). Anatomy of a fake news scandal. Retrieved from Rolling Stone: www.rollingstone.com/feature/anatomy-of-a-fake-news-scandal-125877/

Rogow, F. & Scheibe, C. (n.d.). *NAMLE key questions to ask when analyzing media messages.* Retrieved from NAMLE: https://namle.net/wp-content/uploads/2020/10/NAMLE-Key-Qs.pdf

Rufo, C. [@realchrisrufo]. (2020, August 20). *I will not rest until we have achieved total victory. My goal is simple: to persuade the President of the* [Tweet]. Retrieved from Twitter: https://twitter.com/realchrisrufo/status/1296534425161748480

Sasse, B. (2018). *Them: Why we hate each other—and how to heal.* New York: St. Martin's Press.

Schwartz, S., & Pendharkar, E. (2022, February 2). *Here's the long list of topics Republicans want banned from the classroom.* Retrieved from EdWeek: www.edweek.org/policy-politics/heres-the-long-list-of-topics-republicans-want-banned-from-the-classroom/2022/02

Shapiro, S., & Brown, C. (2018). *The state of civics education.* Center for American Progress. Retrieved from Center for American Progress: www.americanprogress.org/article/state-civics-education/

Sheasley, C. (2022, January 28). *Teaching race in schools: Have these moms found a way forward?* Retrieved from Christian Science Monitor: www.csmonitor.com/layout/set/print/USA/Education/2022/0128/Teaching-race-in-schools-Have-these-moms-found-a-way-forward

Shigeoka, S., & Marsh, J. (2020, July 22). Eight keys to bridging our differences. Retrieved from Greater Good Magazine: https://greatergood.berkeley.edu/article/item/eight_keys_to_bridging_our_differences

Shorr, K. (2021, May 25). Personal interview. (K. Lenci, Interviewer)

Smith, A., & Smith, J. A. (2021, January 4). Six techniques to help you bridge differences. Retrieved from Greater Good Magazine: https://greatergood.berkeley.edu/article/item/six_techniques_to_help_you_bridge_differences?utm_campaign=0ba3e2abbf-EMAIL_CAMPAIGN_FEBRUARY_2021_calendar&utm_medium=email&utm_source=Greater%20Good%20Science%20Center&utm_term=0_5ae73e326e-0ba3e2abbf-742799

Sonmez, F. (2021, November 9). GOP Rep. Fred Upton receives death threats after voting for bipartisan infrastructure deal. Retrieved from Washington Post: www.washingtonpost.com/politics/gop-rep-fred-upton-receives-death-threats-after-voting-for-bipartisan-infrastructure-deal/2021/11/09/78fe5ac8-4195-11ec-9ea7-3eb2406a2e24_story.html

Staff, P. (2021, February 28). *Ask a negotiation expert: How conversational receptiveness might bridge our divide.* Retrieved from Program on Negotiation, Harvard Law School: www.pon.harvard.edu/daily/negotiation-skills-daily/ask-a-negotiation-expert-how-conversational-receptiveness-might-bridge-our-divide-nb/

Stelter, B. (2020, September 6). *Analysis: Fox News segment prompts Trump to target diversity training.* Retrieved from CNN: www.cnn.com/2020/09/06/media/donald-trump-fox-news-critical-race-theory/index.html

Stone, D., & Heen, S. (2014). *Thanks for the feedback.* New York: Penguin Books.

Tajfel, H., Billig, M., Bundy, R., & Flament, C. (1971). Social categorization and intergroup behaviour. *European Journal of Social Psychology, 1*(2), 149–178.

Tangle. (n.d.). Retrieved from Tangle: www.readtangle.com/about

The Aspen Institute. (2018). *From a nation at risk to a nation at hope.* Retrieved from The Aspen Institute National Commission on Social, Emotional, & Academic Development: http://nationathope.org/wp-content/uploads/2018_aspen_final-report_full_webversion.pdf

The Better Arguments Project. (2020). *Our approach.* Retrieved from Better Arguments Project: https://betterarguments.org/our-approach/

The Better Arguments Project. (2020). *Our resources.* Retrieved from Better Arguments Project: https://betterarguments.org/resources-tabs/#education

The Flip Side. (n.d.). Retrieved from The Flip Side: www.theflipside.io/

Turner, L. (2022, February 17). Personal interview. (K. Lenci, Interviewer)

United States Holocaust Memorial Museum. (2012). *Martin Niemoller: "First They Came for the Socialists…."* Retrieved from United States Holocaust Memorial Museum: https://encyclopedia.ushmm.org/content/en/article/martin-niemoeller-first-they-came-for-the-socialists van Boven, L., Ehret, P., & Sherman, D. (2018). Psychological barriers to bipartisan public support for climate policy. *Perspectives on Psychological Science*, *13*(4), 492–507.

Vasilogambros, M. (2021, June 11). *After Capitol riot, some states turn to civics education*. Retrieved from The Current: https://thecurren tga.org/2021/06/11/after-capitol-riot-some-states-turn-to-civics-education/

von Glahn, R. (2020). Civility, citizenship education, and the challenges in a school community setting. Retrieved from Independent Teacher: www.nais.org/magazine/independent-teacher/spring-2020/civility-citizenship-education-and-the-challenges-in-a-sch ool-community-setting/

Waytz, A., Young, L. L., & Ginges, J. (2014). Motive attribution asym-metry for love vs. hate drives intractable conflict. *Proceedings of the National Academy of Sciences*, *111*(44), 15687–15692.

Worland, J. (2017, July 27). Climate change used to be a bipartisan issue. Here's what changed. Retrieved from Time: https://time.com/4874 888/climate-change-politics-history/

Yudkin, D., Hawkins, S., & Dixon, T. (2019). *The perception gap: How false impressions are pulling Americans apart.* New York: More in Common.

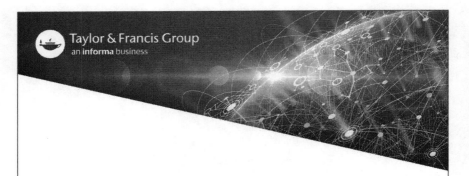

Made in the USA
Coppell, TX
10 June 2024